# YANKEE STADIUM

## A TRIBUTE

### 85 YEARS OF MEMORIES: 1923-2008

WITH COMMENTARY BY THREE GENERATIONS OF YANKEES

INCLUDES ORIGINAL DVD DOCUMENTARY

HOSTED BY REGGIE JACKSON

## LES KRANTZ

Harper
Entertainment
*An Imprint of HarperCollins Publishers*

# Acknowledgements

The author is especially grateful to the contributing writers listed below and to HarperCollins Editor Mauro DiPreta for his amazing suggestions and his knowledge of baseball and books. It was a priviledge to work with such professionals. To David Aretha who wrote most of the script for the documentary, Jack Piantino and Kristie Back for their superb video editing of our documentary on the DVD, and to Show Host Reggie Jackson and Matt Merola who put us together. Thanks too to Tim Knight, Manuscript Editor and our designers listed below. Others whose help and support was appreciated are: Marcia Schiff, Jennifer Schulkind, Sara Bower, Ben Harry, Bob Wolff and Rick Wolff. And to so many Yankees who contributed commentary for this book including (in alphapetical order): Yogi Berra, Johny Blanchard, Jerry Coleman, Whitey Ford, Derek Jeter, Don Larsen, Don Mattingly, Bobby Murcer, Graig Nettles, Bobby Richardson, Dave Righetti, Moose Skowron, Mel Stottlemyre, Joe Torre, Tom Tresh, and Bob Turley.

---

Contributing Writers: Paul Adomites, Bill Chastain, David Fischer, Dave Kaplan

All photos are from AP Worldwide, except the following: Corbis: 21, 55, 59, 63, 83, 84 right, 147. Getty Images: 54, 76 top and bottom, 108, 110 top and bottom, 114 bottom, 116 top, 130, 131, 135, 137, 142, 160.

FIRST EDITION

Produced by: Facts That Matter, Inc.
Jacket Designed by: Les Krantz
Interior Designed by: Julie Shimer and Kris Grauvogl
Page Composition by: Nei-Turner Media Group, Inc.

Library of Congress Cataloging-in-Publication Data is available upon request.
ISBN: 978-0-06-143860-8

08  09  10  11  12  /RRD  10  9  8  7  6  5  4  3  2  1

# Preface

As the Roaring '20s began, the Yankees needed to build a new stadium because Babe Ruth's drawing power exceeding the capacity of the Polo Grounds, the home field of both the Yankees since 1913, and the National League's New York Giants since 1911. But with Ruth blasting a record 54 homers in 1920, almost doubling his previous record of 29, the Yankees attracted a whopping 1,289,422 fans—more than the Giants themselves drew. Miffed, the Giants informed their guests to vacate the premises as soon as possible.

Yankee owners Jacob Ruppert and Tillinghast l'Hommedieu Huston happily obliged. Early in 1921, they announced that the team had purchased 10 acres of land in the west Bronx as the site of the Yankees' new home, a triple-decked, 70,000-seat "stadium"—the first ballpark to be designated as such. It would be roofed all the way around, making it, according to a press release, "impenetrable to all human eyes, save those of aviators." However, this bowl-shaped design was eventually abandoned.

---

Two weeks before construction began, Ruppert bought Huston's share of the Yankees for $1.5 million. The White Construction Company began work on May 5, 1922. For $2.5 million, the company had agreed to construct Yankee Stadium by Opening Day of the following season. Amazingly, they achieved the feat. Yankee Stadium, at 800 Ruppert Place, opened on April 18, 1923.

Builders maintained the triple-deck design, but not all the way around the stadium. The outfield was left open, treating fans to sunlight and a view of the city. The original park accommodated the envisioned 70,000 fans, as evidenced by the 74,200 who sardined themselves into the park for the very first game. Together, they shared the stadium's 16 restrooms—considered an ample amount at the time.

While visitors were impressed by the roof's copper façade, many were perplexed about the outfield dimensions: 280 feet in left, 500 in deep left-center, 487 to straightaway center, 350 to right-center, and 295 down the right-field line. At least the oddly shaped field would favor Ruth, a pull-hitting, left-handed slugger.

Over the next 50 years, the Yankees tinkered with the stadium's design numerous times. In the 1920s and '30s, the grandstands were extended to the outfield, enclosing the stadium to a greater degree while upping the number of seats. Seating capacity changed a dozen times, with a high of 82,000 in 1927. Numerous changes were made to the outfield: Concrete bleachers replaced wooden ones; chairs replaced outfield bench seats; auxiliary scoreboards were constructed in the late 1940s. Many of these changes affected the dimensions of the outfield fence.

Eventually, the once-magnificent stadium fell into disrepair. By the early 1970s, with attendance sagging, everyone agreed that Yankee Stadium needed a major overhaul. The House That Ruth Built closed for repairs in 1974 and '75, forcing the Yankees to bunk up with another cross-town rival, Shea Stadium's New York Mets.

In 2008, the House That Ruth built will close forever, being replaced by a more modern stadium across the street. Never again shall we lay eyes on the same playing field where the Sultan of Swat wowed the fans; where Lou Gehrig, the luckiest man in the world, won our admiration; where Joe DiMaggio swung his mighty club; and where pitchers named Larsen, Cone, and Wells reached pure perfection. Not only will the original Yankee Stadium continue to live in our hearts, it will live in immortality. Surely it will be regarded by all who have entered its portals as the greatest ballpark in the history of baseball—and the greatest sports venue of all time. Old friend, we will miss you!

LES KRANTZ

44

70

90

110

162

167

*Part 1*

# *Magical Moments*

# The Babe Wallops a Record 60

## September 20, 1927

In the eighth inning, Ruth socked a low, inside fastball into the right-field bleachers for his record 60th home run. Washington pitcher Tom Zachary cried "foul ball," but it was fair by a foot.

**Opposite Page:** Ruth and Lou Gehrig demolished MLB's teammate record for home runs by knocking 107 out of the park in 1927. Shortly after the season, they donned these uniforms for a western barnstorming tour.

The House That Ruth Built is the most lasting of the many nicknames accorded Yankee Stadium over the years. And for good reason—nobody was better than Ruth at filling the seats of that stadium or the Polo Grounds, where the Yankees played before the advent of Yankee Stadium. Ruth drew fans like ants to a picnic.

Ruth's 1927 season is one reason why so many wanted to push through the turnstiles to see the Sultan of Swat hit one of his tremendous home runs. Not only did he hit long ones, but he hit plenty of them. In 1921, he established an American League record—breaking his own mark of 54 set in 1920—by hitting 59 homers. But succeeding years saw him hit 35, 41, 46, 25, and 47, making the 50 Home run plateau appear to be a far away land that Ruth could no longer reach.

Still, Ruth reigned as the best player in the major leagues. Not only had he belted 47 home runs in 1926, but he also hit .372. And, heading into 1927, Ruth and the sports world knew that he would be hitting in the middle of what many believe to be the most powerful lineup in baseball history. Among this collection of hitters were Bob Meusel, Earle Combs, Tony Lazzeri, and the amazing Lou Gehrig, otherwise collectively known as Murderer's Row.

Heading into the final month of the season, Ruth appeared as though he would once again breathe the magic air of 50 home runs, as he had accrued 43 by the end of August. Nobody expected what happened next.

Ruth began to hit home runs like never before. September belonged to the Bambino, and his home run total climbed. With four games left, he had 56 home runs. Number 57, a grand slam, came in game 151 of the 155-game season (one tie had to be replayed). In the Yankees' next game against the Senators, he hit his 58th and 59th homers in a game where he flirted with four home runs. Unfortunately for Ruth, one of the hits went to the deep right-center field, where it hit the bottom of the wall. By the time the Senators returned the ball to the infield, Ruth had made it to third base with a triple. Had he pulled the ball even a little, it would have left the playing field. In his final at-bat, Ruth hit a deep drive to right field that came up a couple of feet short before being caught. The calendar now showed two games

Though he indulged in the New York high life, Ruth also enjoyed spending time with children. Here, he mesmerizes youngsters with tales of his life, including his years at St. Mary's Industrial School for Boys.

In addition to his chart-topping 60 homers in 1927, Ruth led the AL in runs (158), walks (137), slugging (.772), and OBP (.486).

remaining in the season, and Ruth's ledger showed him one home run shy of 60.

The Yankees had 108 wins to their credit, with two games remaining, when they hosted the Senators at Yankee Stadium. They had already won the pennant, and the World Series sat on the horizon. Only one question remained in the thoughts of those sitting in the stands and dugouts at the hallowed ballpark: Can he do it? Could Ruth reach 60 home runs?

By the time he stepped to the plate in the eighth inning, Ruth had walked, collected a single to deep right field in the fourth inning, and cracked another single in the sixth. Suspense filled the ballpark when Senators pitcher Tom Zachary looked in for the sign. In all likelihood this at-bat would be Ruth's last chance to break his home run record, at least for that day.

Ruth took a called strike on the first pitch before taking one at the letters to make the count 1-1. Surely Ruth would go down swinging in an attempt to knock one out of the park.

Zachary delivered his third pitch. A fastball came in low and inside. Ruth took a huge swing. He did not miss. Nobody in Yankee Stadium had any doubts that the ball had the distance to reach the right-field seats; only the accuracy of the drive was in doubt, as it curled toward foul territory. The ball landed a foot inside the right-field foul line and midway to the top of the bleachers.

"Foul ball! Foul ball!" Zachary yelled, arguing with the umpire to no avail.

Ruth rounded the bases much to the approval of the unusually sparse crowd of approximately 10,000, which tossed confetti and hats into the air. The salute continued when Ruth ran out to right field in the top of the ninth, as the crowd waved handkerchiefs. Ruth basked in the attention.

"Sixty," the Babe would say later. "Count 'em, 60. Let's see some other SOB match that."

A crowd of 20,000 showed up at Yankee Stadium the next day, hoping to see Ruth add one more to his new home run record. Unfortunately, he went 0-for-3, with a strikeout in his final at-bat of the regular season, to leave the single-season home run mark at 60—a high bar that would not be broken until three decades later, when Yankee Roger Maris famously broke the record.

"Babe Ruth was the greatest ever, he created the whole mystique of Yankee Stadium."

—Tom Tresh

## The Heart of the Order

Babe Ruth brought the home run into fashion when he hit an unprecedented 29 in 1919; and then went to 54 in 1920 and 59 in 1921.

Prior to Ruth, home runs were not really a part of the game, and were viewed as more of a freak occurrence. The fields were much bigger then and the balls softer. As time wore on, a harder ball and more stadiums with outfield stands—which were easier to reach—helped make for more home runs. Still, Ruth remained the man when it came to four-baggers. Nobody in the game could hit home runs like the Bambino. That is until 1927.

Lou Gehrig, who batted behind Ruth in the Yankees' order, went toe-to-toe with Ruth in home runs during the summer of 1927. Newspapers referred to the friendly competition for the home run title as the "Great American Home run Derby."

The competition reached a crescendo September 5 in Boston, when Gehrig homered to tie Ruth at 44. Some wondered if Gehrig really could dethrone his teammate, who was by then an American icon. Ruth answered the challenge on September 6, with three home runs against the Red Sox; the following day he hit two more to effectively leave Gehrig in the rear-view mirror en route to his record-setting 60-home run season.

Gehrig finished the season with a career-high 49 home runs, but far short of Ruth. However, the Iron Horse did not seem bothered by all the attention Ruth received. As Gehrig later said, "I'm not a headline guy. I know that as long as I was following Babe Ruth to the plate I could have stood on my head and no one would have known the difference."

# DiMaggio Streaks to 56

## May 15 - July 16, 1941

Joe McCarthy congratulates Joe D. after he hit safely in his 42nd game, on June 29 at Washington. The hit broke George Sisler's modern MLB record of 41 games, set in 1922.

**Opposite Page:** DiMaggio ties Wee Willie Keeler's major-league record with a hit in his 44th consecutive game, on July 1 against Boston. He shattered the record the next day with a blast into the left-field seats.

The news was nothing but grim in the spring of '41. Hitler's forces had overrun much of Europe, including France, and were bombing Britain on a daily basis. The United States had yet to enter the war, but defense plants were operating seven days week.

Though in need of an escape from the bleak reports, New Yorkers could find little solace in their Yankees. When the team lost 13-1 to Chicago on May 15, its record stood at 14-15. "Yank Attack Weakest in Years," declared the *New York Journal American*. Yet barely noticed that afternoon was a hit by 26-year-old Yankees star Joe DiMaggio. His single launched a two-month-long hitting streak that erupted into a national phenomenon and—for brief periods each day—provided much-needed relief from the realities of war.

DiMaggio had struggled early in the season, but his bat came alive against the White Sox. On May 16, he blasted a triple and a homer in a 6-5 Yankees win. "After the streak started," said teammate Phil Rizzuto, "he hit nothing but bullets. Even the outs were ripped. I was glad I didn't have to play the infield in front of him, because he hit shots that took off your glove and your hand along with it."

The streak almost ended at 15 games on May 30. But when Red Sox outfielder Pete Fox lost DiMaggio's ball in the sun, it fell for a double. On June 2, Joltin' Joe managed two hits off Cleveland ace Bob Feller to stretch the streak to 19. Though DiMaggio's hot hitting had yet to capture the nation's attention, it was boosting the Yankees lineup. Beginning June 7, New York won 40 of 46 games (en route to 101 wins and the world title). Said Yankees outfielder Tommy Henrich, "He was a one-man gang who brought our whole doggone ballclub together." And the hits just kept on coming. On June 16, DiMaggio tied the team record held by Roger Peckinpaugh and Earle Combs by hitting in 29 straight games. The next day at the stadium, official scorer Dan Daniel awarded Joe a hit after his grounder caromed off the shoulder of White Sox shortstop Luke Appling.

The streak was now 30, and DiMaggio was the toast of the town. When he attended the Joe Louis–Billy Conn fight at the Polo Grounds on June 18, "he nearly started a riot," said his friend, George Solotaire. "There were so many people asking for his autograph that he

"Joe had an imperial presence. Somebody once asked him why he played so hard, even when we were so far ahead. He said because somebody who never saw him play may be watching for the first time. He always felt he had to prove his greatness."

—Jerry Coleman

had almost as many cops around him as the fighters."

As the streak progressed, Americans became obsessed with the idea of DiMaggio breaking the record—or records. George Sisler had set the modern Major League Baseball mark with 41 straight in 1922. Wee Willie Keeler (whose creed was "hit 'em where they ain't") had authored a 44-game streak in 1897. DiMaggio seemed immune to the pressure—unconcerned that fans by the millions clung to every pitch he faced. "I never really gave the record much thought until I had hit in about 33 or 34 games," he told the *New York Herald Tribune*.

Meanwhile, on June 22, German troops stormed into the Soviet Union, killing Red Army soldiers and innocent civilians by the thousands.

In the States, the excitement of DiMaggio's streak was a welcome distraction. In game 40 at Philadelphia on June 28, Johnny Babich of the A's tried to pitch around DiMaggio, throwing three straight pitches wide of the strike zone. The 3-0 delivery was outside too, but Joltin' Joe drilled it through Babich's legs for a single. A's fans stood and cheered.

In a doubleheader in Washington on June 29, DiMaggio had a chance to tie and break Sisler's record. In the first game, he cracked a double that rolled to the 422-foot sign. In game two, he knocked a single in the seventh inning.

The nation's attention focused on Yankee Stadium on July 1, as the Red Sox were in town for a twin bill. With hits in both games, DiMaggio

would tie Keeler's all-time record of 44 straight games. In the fourth inning of the opener, DiMaggio was awarded a hit on a difficult chance by third baseman Jim Tabor. His clean single in the first inning of the nightcap tied the record.

Prior to the July 2 game, DiMaggio had invited his brother Dom, Boston's center fielder, to his home for dinner that evening. Dom responded by nearly ending the streak, with a spectacular running catch that robbed his brother of extra bases. "It was a great catch," DiMaggio recalled. "One of the best Dom had ever made. I was tempted at that point to withdraw the dinner invitation for the evening."

Later, in the fifth inning, Joe hit one that Dom couldn't reach—into the left-field seats. Amid a raucous ovation, DiMaggio tipped his cap as he trotted to the dugout, where he was swarmed by teammates. "You not only broke Keeler's record," pitcher Lefty Gomez told him, "you even used his formula— you hit 'em where they ain't."

Although the record was broken, the buzz of the streak continued to build. Radio stations interrupted programs with

breaking news from Yankee Stadium. DJs played "Joltin' Joe DiMaggio" by the Les Brown Orchestra over and over. Meanwhile, the Yankee Clipper was hotter than ever, with four-hit games against Philadelphia and St. Louis, and three hits at Cleveland in game 56.

In the next game, on July 17, the run of glory finally ended. Indians third sacker Ken Keltner made two outstanding backhand stops to rob DiMaggio. Had it not rained, which muddied the batter's box, Joe might have beaten out the first of those grounders. He also walked and, in his last at-bat, grounded into a double play. "I can't say I'm glad it's over," DiMaggio said after the game. "Of course, I wanted it to go on as long as it could."

For Yankees fans, and Americans in general, the news of DiMaggio's hitless game was more than disappointing. The excitement of the streak—the daily escape from reality—was gone. Now, the only news was grim. On the last day of the streak, German troops encircled Smolensk, Russia, trapping 600,000 people. In five months, America would enter the war.

DiMaggio and Ted Williams (left), who ripped .406 in 1941, batted third and fourth for the AL in the 1941 All-Star Game. The hot-hitting twosome went a combined 3-for-8 in the game with four runs and five RBI.

Less than five months after DiMaggio's streak ended, Japan bombed Pearl Harbor. Joe was sworn into the army on February 17, 1943, and served 31 months as a physical education instructor.

Exactly 25 years after Ken Keltner robbed him of two hits to end his streak, DiMaggio still can't let it go. Here he playfully chokes the former third baseman on July 23, 1966.

"Seeing Joe DiMaggio the first time was a pretty big thing. I was 21, right out of Purdue, and reported to the instructional camp in Arizona, where the Yankees also had spring training. Hell, I was just thrilled to be wearing the same uniform."

—Moose Skowron

# The Highlights

Over the course of the 56 games, DiMaggio batted .408 with 15 homers, 16 doubles, four triples, 55 RBI, and, appropriately, 56 runs scored. Riding his coattails, the Yankees went 41-13 (with two games called). Here are some highlights:

**Game 1:** Cracked his first hit of the streak off Chicago's Eddie Smith.

**Game 12:** Went 4-for-5 with three runs and three RBI against Washington.

**Game 16:** Kept the streak alive when his routine fly ball was lost in the sun by Red Sox outfielder Pete Fox. DiMaggio made three errors in the game.

**Games 19 and 27:** Laced hits in both games off Indians great Bob Feller.

**Game 23:** Belted two home runs against St. Louis.

**Game 30:** Broke Yankees record of 29 straight games held by Roger Peckinpaugh and Earle Combs, thanks to a favorable ruling by the official scorer.

**Game 32:** Gets just three at-bats against the White Sox, but laces a hit each time up.

**Game 33:** Went 4-for-5 against Detroit.

**Game 38:** Got his first hit with two outs in the ninth at St. Louis. (The previous batter, Tommy Henrich, had bunted to avoid hitting into a game-ending double play.)

**Game 41:** Had his favorite bat stolen after the game. It was later returned.

**Game 42:** Broke George Sisler's modern MLB record of 41 straight games.

**Game 45:** Broke Wee Willie Keeler's all-time MLB record of 44 straight games.

**Game 47:** Cracked four hits versus Philadelphia.

**Game 50:** Went 4-for-5 against St. Louis.

**Game 56:** Went 3-for-4 at Cleveland in the final game of the streak.

**Game 57:** Went hitless against the Indians, losing out on $10,000 promotional deal from Heinz 57.

**July 18:** A day after his 56-game streak came to a close, DiMaggio began a 16-game hitting streak.

# Reynolds Tosses Double No-Nos

## September 28, 1951

This fireballer didn't become a great pitcher until his 30s, when he learned to change speeds and set up hitters. He went 17-8 in 1951 and 20-8 a year later.

The New York Yankees went into their September 28, 1951, doubleheader against the Red Sox at Yankee Stadium knowing that a sweep would clinch the American League pennant. Starting the first game of the twin bill would be Allie Reynolds, who had enjoyed a fine season for the Yankees.

Reynolds was in his fifth season as a Yankee, courtesy of the famed Yankee Clipper, Joe DiMaggio, who had suggested to the Yankees' management that Reynolds would be a terrific acquisition, despite his 11-15 record for the Cleveland Indians in 1946. The Oklahoma native had paid rich dividends, posting a 68-33 record for the Yankees in the four seasons heading into the 1951 campaign.

Up until the final day of the 1951 season, the 6-foot, 190-pound right-hander's defining moment had occurred earlier in the season on July 12. That day, Cleveland's Municipal Stadium hosted a crowd of 39,195 fans, who watched Reynolds outduel Indians ace Bob Feller en route to pitching a 1-0 no-hitter. Feller had already accrued the third no-hitter of his career just over a week earlier, and it looked like he might throw his fourth when he went toe-to-toe with Reynolds. Mickey Mantle finally ended Feller's bid with one out in the sixth. Gene Woodling's home run an inning later held up as the only run of the game.

Meanwhile, Reynolds, known as "Chief" due to his Indian heritage, continued to mow down Cleveland. The Indians managed just four base runners—three on walks and one on an error by Yankees shortstop Phil Rizzuto in the first inning—but none reached on a hit, while Reynolds struck out four en route to a 1-0 win and his first ever no-hitter. Reynolds' gem was the first Yankees no-hitter since Monte Pearson no-hit the Indians at Yankee Stadium in 1938.

On September 28, Reynolds started the first game of a doubleheader at Yankee Stadium against the Red Sox, his team's postseason fate in his hands.

Reynolds overpowered the Red Sox through the first eight innings without allowing a hit. Excitement and tension rippled through the Yankee Stadium stands when Reynolds strolled to the mound in the top of the ninth. All hoped to see Reynolds accomplish the unlikely.

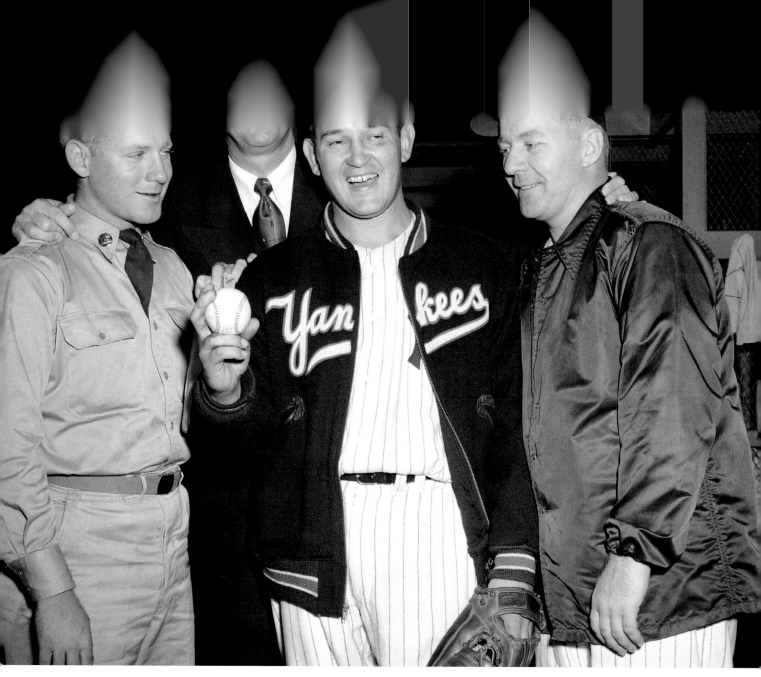

Yankees pitcher Whitey Ford (left), on leave from the army in 1951, was among those who congratulated Reynolds. Allie became just the second big-league pitcher to toss two no-hitters in the same season.

The Yankees led 8-0, so Reynolds had his 17th win of the season well in hand. Could he get three more outs without giving up a hit?

Reynolds retired the first two batters of the inning to bring Ted Williams to the plate.

Reynolds had struck out nine while walking four for the afternoon. No Red Sox hitter got close to hitting the ball well, and none reached second base. But this was Ted Williams. A second no-hitter hinged upon retiring the Splendid Splinter, who hit .318, fourth best in the American League that season, and who would win six batting titles during his career.

A collective sigh of relief could be heard throughout the stadium when Reynolds got Williams to hit a high pop-up behind home plate. Yogi Berra camped under the ball as it fell from the sky, but the Yankees catcher inexplicably dropped the ball when it hit his glove. Frustrated, Berra dropped to the turf and Williams was born again.

Throughout the history of baseball, such miscues had proved to be costly, yet Reynolds took the setback in stride. Patting Berra on the back and offering encouragement, Reynolds told him, "Don't worry, Yogi, we'll get him again." He then went back to work.

Reynolds once again got Williams to pop up. Berra didn't miss it this time around; he hauled in the pop-up in front of the Yankees' dugout for the final out of a masterpiece. Reynolds had recorded his second no-hitter of the season to become the second player in major-league history to throw two no-hitters in one season. (Johnny Vander Meer had been the first when he pitched back-to-back no-hitters for the Cincinnati Reds in 1938.) The victory assured the Yankees of a tie for the American

League pennant. When they won the second game of the doubleheader 11-3, they clinched the pennant, which seemed a little anticlimactic, considering Reynolds' feat in the first game.

Thanks to Reynolds, the Yankees went on to defeat the New York Giants in the World Series to win their third consecutive championship.

**Opposite Page:** Reynolds savors a moment alone with the ball that earned him immortality. His next start would be Game 1 of the World Series against the Giants, who were coming off the "Shot Heard 'Round the World."

The Yankees swarm Reynolds after his second no-hitter.

## Yankee Stadium No-Hitters

**August 27, 1938:** Monte Pearson defeats Cleveland, 13-0

**April 30, 1946:** Bob Feller (Cleveland) defeats Yankees, 1-0

**September 28, 1951:** Allie Reynolds defeats Boston, 8-0

**August 25, 1952:** Virgil Trucks (Detroit) defeats Yankees, 1-0

**October 8, 1956:** Don Larsen throws a perfect game to defeat Brooklyn, 2-0, in the World Series

**July 4, 1983:** Dave Righetti defeats Boston, 4-0

**September 4, 1993:** Jim Abbott defeats Cleveland, 4-0

**May 14, 1996:** Dwight Gooden defeats Seattle, 2-0

**May 17, 1998:** David Wells throws a perfect game to beat Minnesota, 4-0

**July 18, 1999:** David Cone tosses a perfect game to overwhelm Montreal, 6-0

**June 11, 2003:** Six Houston Astros pitchers (Roy Oswalt, Peter Munro, Kirk Saarloos, Brad Lidge [winning pitcher], Octavio Dotel, and Billy Wagner) defeat Yankees, 8-0

# The Mick's Mighty Blast

## May 30, 1956

After a 1953 game, the Mick shows how he almost hit the cover off the ball. Fans and physicists often wondered how he could generate so much power from his 5'11", 198-pound frame.

**Opposite Page:** These diagrams show the two balls that Mantle smashed against Washington on May 30. The drive on the right came within 18 inches of becoming the first ball ever to escape Yankee Stadium.

Many legends have been born at Yankee Stadium through extraordinary athletic feats. Mickey Mantle is one such legend, and the events of May 30, 1956, added to the magnitude of that legend.

Never had a baseball prospect been more highly touted than Mantle when the 19-year-old arrived in New York in 1951. A raw-boned country boy from Commerce, Oklahoma, Mantle could hit, run, and throw, but it was his power that set him apart. Few in the history of the game could match Mantle in that department, and he could hit home runs of epic distance from either side of the plate.

At the age of 17, Mantle hit three home runs in a game playing for a team in Baxter Springs, Kansas. The last of the blows landed in a river over 500 feet away. So from the first time Mantle stepped on the turf at Yankee Stadium, he bore the proverbial weight of the world on his shoulders, trying to live up to expectations. And the pressure from Mantle's situation showed in his performance. While nothing could hide the brilliant skills of the youngster wearing No. 7, he wasn't reaching anywhere near peak performance. Yankees fans reminded Mantle daily that he was not Joe DiMaggio. Some wondered if he ever would reach the unrealistic potential level forecast for him. Nevertheless, Mantle survived, and the passage of time brought Yankees fans to his side. After all, nobody could deny his charm, his speed, and his power.

In June of 1955, he hit a ball off Kansas City Athletics left-hander Alex Kellner that cleared the wall in center field, just to the right of the 461-foot mark. Estimates calculated the blast to be 486 feet. That summer, he also hit one against the White Sox at Comiskey Park that measured 550 feet.

By 1956, Mantle was no longer considered a kid, but the best player in the Yankees' lineup, and perhaps the best player in baseball—a claim he validated daily from the start of the season.

Using Hank Bauer's 32-ounce bat from the left side of the plate and Moose Skowron's 36-ounce bat from the right side, Mantle carried a hot streak into the doubleheader against

"Being a pitcher who used to face Mickey, I was in shock when he hit the ball. Nobody, but nobody hit it harder or longer. I remember him batting left-handed once; he broke his bat and still hit it over 380 feet for a homer. He was unbelievable."

—Bob Turley

"I used to kid Mickey, it didn't matter how far he hit 'em, they only counted as one. But that one off [Pedro] Ramos that nearly cleared the stadium, maybe that should've counted for two."

—Yogi Berra

Mantle displays three bats and a crown after winning the Triple Crown (tops in the league in batting average, homers, and RBI) in 1956. Meanwhile, Casey Stengel raves about his pupil's talents, as he often did.

**Opposite Page:** On April 17, 1953, Mantle's shot left the building at Washington's Griffith Stadium. Measured at 565 feet, it became the "official" record for the longest ball ever hit.

MICKEY MANTLE'S TITANIC 565 FOOT HOME RUN

HIT RIGHT-HANDED, FIFTH INNING, AGAINST WASHINGTON SENATORS, CHUCK STOBBS PITCHING, GRIFFITH STADIUM, APRIL 17, 1953

the Washington Senators at Yankee Stadium on May 30. He had hit his 18th homer of the season the day before against the Red Sox—his 14th during the month of May alone. The blast had put him nine games ahead of Babe Ruth's pace when he set the single-season home run record of 60 in 1927.

A crowd of 29,825 fans at Yankee Stadium cheered Mantle when he stepped to the plate in the fifth inning of the opening game of the doubleheader. Pedro Ramos stood on the mound for the Senators, bringing an odd look to hitters with his right-handed submarine delivery. Mantle, batting left-handed, fought the count to 2-2, and then connected, sending a majestic blast to right field. The ball continued to rise and appeared as though it might become the first fair ball to ever leave Yankee Stadium. But the drive didn't quite have enough space to leave the stadium completely, hitting the façade, only 18 inches short of clearing the roof. The ball struck an area some 370 feet away from home plate, approximately 117 feet above the playing field, before ricocheting back onto the grass.

Throughout the history of Major League Baseball, estimates of home run distances have never been an exact science. Harry Heilmann is believed to have hit the longest in baseball history during the 1921 season, when he hit one estimated to be 610 feet at Detroit's Navin Field. Conservative estimates suggest that Mantle's blast could have equaled Heilmann's blow.

"It was the best I ever hit a ball left-handed," Mantle told *The New York Times*.

Mantle added his 20th home run of the season in the second game, which helped pace a 52-home run season for the Yankees slugger, who went on to win the American League's Triple Crown in 1956.

# What Might've Been

Mickey Mantle was the epitome of the five-tool player. He could run, hit for power, hit for average, throw, and field. Scouts still talk about how Mantle could run from the left side of home plate to first base in an amazing 3.1 seconds, a second faster than the average major leaguer. And while tales of his many tape-measure home runs are the most prominent in his legacy, he truly was an all-around ballplayer.

During the doubleheader against the Senators in which he clouted one of the most memorable home runs in the history of Yankee Stadium, he put on display his other gifts that day as well. Along with the pair of homers, Mantle added a drag bunt single, a line-drive single, a stolen base, a walk, and an assist.

Ironically, as good as Mantle was, he never played in top physical shape while in the major leagues, thanks to the first World Series he played in as a 19-year-old in 1951, when the Yankees played the New York Giants.

On October 5, 1951, Game 2 took place at Yankee Stadium. Mantle was playing right field and Joe DiMaggio center when Willie Mays hit a fly ball that both chased. When DiMaggio called the ball, Mantle braced to give way to DiMaggio, and caught his spikes on a drainage outlet; the resulting injury to his right knee brought Mantle's season to an abrupt, painful end. Mantle went on to have a Hall of Fame career, but one has to wonder what might have been had he not severely damaged his knee.

# Maris One-Ups the Babe

## October 1, 1961

When Claire Ruth, Babe's widow, arrived at Yankee Stadium on August 16 for Babe Ruth League Day, it was only natural that she posed with Mantle and Maris. Roger belted two homers that day, giving him 48 to Mickey's 45.

**Opposite Page:** Maris cracks the home run that beat the Babe—a fourth-inning smash that sailed 360 feet into the right-field seats. Tracy Stallard had left a 2-0 fastball over too much of the plate.

The 1961 season was one of many changes in the American League. The Washington Senators moved to Minnesota, and the Los Angeles Angels and a new Washington Senators team joined the circuit.

Along with the expansion of teams, the schedule was expanded from 154 to 162 games. That season, Yankee's sluggers Mickey Mantle and Roger Maris both took aim at Babe Ruth's single-season home run record of 60 in 1927. With eight extra games added to the schedule, baseball commissioner Ford Frick ruled on July 17 that any new mark would be listed as a separate record entirely, unless it was set before the 155th game. His official proclamation read, in part, "If the player does not hit more than 60 until after his club has played 154 games, there would have to be some distinctive mark in the record books to show that Babe Ruth's record was set under a 154-game schedule and the total of more than 60 was compiled while a 162-game schedule was in effect." Frick, by the way, had been Babe Ruth's biographer, business partner, and drinking buddy.

At the end of August, Maris had 51 home runs and Mantle 48. Yankees fans appeared to be pulling for the homegrown Mantle to break the record, rather than Maris, who had been acquired from Kansas City prior to the previous season. During September, Mantle came down with an injury and he ended up hitting 54, leaving it to Maris to continue the chase of Ruth's record.

An intensely private man, Maris was subjected to withering scrutiny by both fans and the media, who didn't want to see Ruth's record fall. He was booed by some fans at the stadium, and on the road as well.

As for the press, reporters dubbed Maris the "angry king of swat" and referred to his "intimidating demeanor." When not asking him the same, inane questions over and over, or criticizing him for not being Babe Ruth, the press concocted a feud between Maris and Mantle, whom they portrayed as bitter rivals. The fact is, they were roommates, and while Maris didn't seek the nightlife the way Mantle did, their lifestyle differences didn't affect either their clubhouse attitude or their play on the field. Although the pressure rattled the

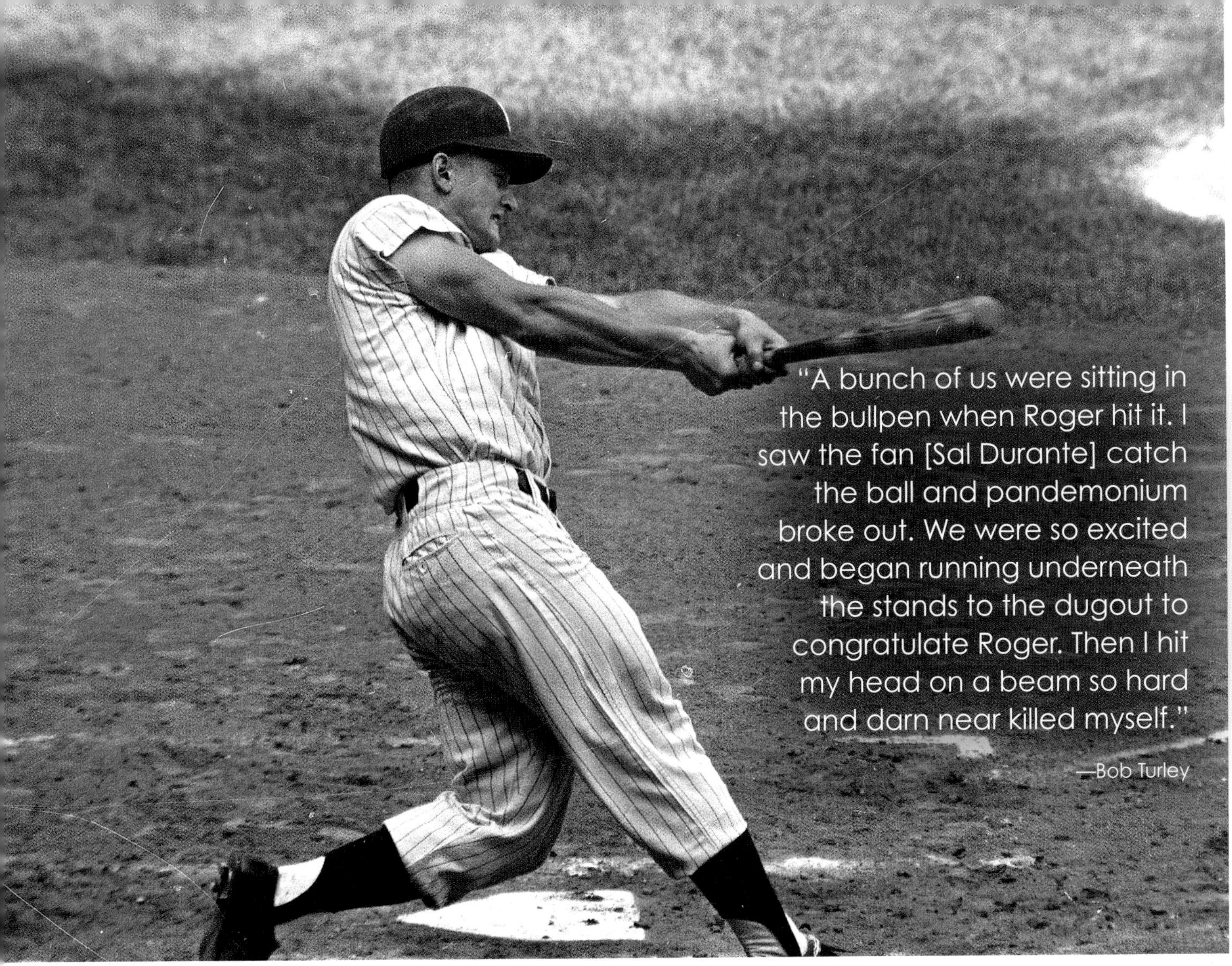

"A bunch of us were sitting in the bullpen when Roger hit it. I saw the fan [Sal Durante] catch the ball and pandemonium broke out. We were so excited and began running underneath the stands to the dugout to congratulate Roger. Then I hit my head on a beam so hard and darn near killed myself."

—Bob Turley

otherwise taciturn Maris to the point that his hair began falling out in clumps, the young man nevertheless hit his 59th home run in game 154 and tied Ruth's record four games later.

On October 1, 1961, only 23,154 fans were on hand to watch Roger Maris' last chance to become the first player ever to top 60 home runs in a single season. It was an unusually modest crowd for the House That Ruth Built, a venue that led the American League in attendance that season, when sellout crowds would fill the stadium's capacity of 67,337. While one lucky fan could come away with the souvenir ball if Maris did manage to hit his 61st—a ball that a California businessman had said he would purchase for a whopping $5,000 should history be made—it wasn't enough incentive to drive fans into the bleachers.

And certainly there were many longtime Yankees fans who did not want to see the number 60 surpassed by anyone—not even another pinstriped slugger. Baseball veterans objected, too. "Maris has no right to break Ruth's record," Hall of Famer Rogers Hornsby told *The New York Times*, summing up the feelings of many who considered themselves baseball purists.

At the outset, the afternoon of October 1 lacked that big-game buzz. Determined not to be remembered as the team that gave Maris his historic blast, the Boston Red Sox had not given him anything to swing at in the series' previous two games. The visitors had long been eliminated from the pennant race, while the Yankees entered the finale with a 108-53 record, knowing they would be facing Cincinnati in the World Series.

25

Maris looks older than his 27 years as he stares back at a photographer on September 30. Maris was under so much stress that he took the Yankees' 160th game off to go shopping.

**Opposite Page:** Maris meets truck driver Sal Durante, age 19, who caught the 61st home run ball. Durante offered Roger the ball, but an equally gracious Maris told him to keep it.

The Red Sox sent 24-year-old Tracy Stallard to the mound to finish his first full season in the major leagues. The right-hander from Virginia pitched well, coaxing Maris to hit a harmless fly ball to left field on an outside pitch in the first inning. Nor did Stallard have much trouble with the other top hitters—men like Bobby Richardson, Yogi Berra, and Moose Skowron—in the New York lineup for most of the day. In fact, the way Stallard was locating his pitches, it became clear early in the game that Maris would probably not be stepping into the Yankee Stadium batter's box more than four times. He needed to capitalize on one of his next three opportunities.

Though no one saw his record-setting 1961 season coming, Maris was no Cinderella story. He had provided many Yankee Stadium thrills the previous season, his first in New York, when he hit 39 home runs, won his first of two American League MVP awards, and helped power the club to another pennant. He and Mickey Mantle gave the Bronx Bombers the most devastating one-two, middle-of-the-order punch in baseball, although the more outgoing Mantle was clearly the fan favorite.

Still, despite the reverence for Ruth's record and the universal love for Mantle, Maris was no villain in Yankee Stadium's confines. Fans booed the young Stallard when he started his fourth-inning battle with Maris by delivering a pitch high and outside. His next offering was low and in for ball two, as the boos intensified in volume. By now, the fans were making it loudly known that Maris deserved a chance.

Stallard's third pitch was one of the few mistakes he made that day. It bit off too much of the plate, at a perfect height for Maris to make contact. Looking for a fastball on that 2-0 count and seeing

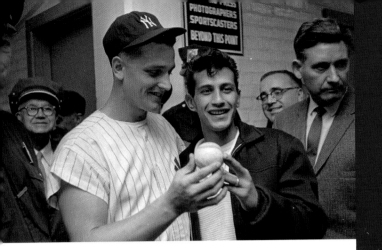

one belt-high, the Yankees slugger began his fluid, left-handed swing and connected. It was not his best stroke of the season; nor did he catch the ball perfectly. Still, it was hit well enough to clear the head of running Red Sox right fielder Lou Clinton, traveling some 360 feet before crashing into the lower-deck bleachers, triggering a mad scramble for the ball. It was the only run Stallard allowed all day in his 1-0 defeat.

Yankee Stadium roared as Maris galloped into his home run trot. He slapped hands with a young fan who had raced onto the field as he rounded third base, and then with third-base coach Frank Crosetti. "Another standing ovation for Roger Maris!" shouted Yankees play-by-play man Phil Rizzuto. "And they want Maris to come out and take another bow."

Given his reserved nature, Maris probably would not have taken a Yankee Stadium curtain call that day had he not been prodded. His teammates were not about to let him sit quietly in the dugout while 23,154 fans—minus the few who were still battling in the right-field seats for the ball—made the noise of 50,000 or more.

"They wanted him to come back out," Mantle said. "He wouldn't come out, so the players … forced him to come out and take a bow. That's the kind of guy he was."

There never was an actual asterisk by Maris' record. It was, however, noted apart from Ruth's mark in the record book until 1991, when a major-league committee voted to recognize Maris as the sole holder of the single-season home run record.

"Maybe I wasn't the chosen one," Maris said, years later, "but I was the one who got the record."

## Asterisks & Other Tomfoolery

When Frick made his pronouncement, he made no mention of an asterisk in the record books if Maris or Mantle reached or passed Ruth in Games 155 or above. But somehow that became what most people thought. Actually, there was no "official" record book, so any publisher of such a book could designate the record however he or she wished. (*The Sporting News* listed two titles, one for 154-game seasons, one for 162-game years.) Frick's edict was just a cranky way of saying that Ruth would always be the best, in his opinion. It lacked any official status. Except that it came from the mouth of the Commish.

One New York writer, Arthur Daley, pointed out that with Babe averaging a homer every 11.8 at-bats, "any fair-minded person" would expect three more if he had played a 162-game season. "Maybe it would have been more because he was phenomenally hot in September."

But Maris did not have that large an edge. Yes, he had 590 at-bats to Babe's 540. But in actual plate appearances, Ruth had 692 in 1927; Maris had 698 in 1961.

Clearly, there was nothing cheap about Maris's record. In fact, it would last for 37 years—three more than Babe Ruth's.

# Yankee Doodle Dandy

## July 4, 1983

AL Rookie of the Year in 1981, Dave Righetti overwhelmed batters with a rising fastball, slider, and big-breaking curve. He went 14-8 in 1983 before taking over closer duties in '84.

**Opposite Page:** Righetti celebrates his Fourth of July no-hitter with catcher Butch Wynegar. It was the Yankees' first no-hitter since Don Larsen's perfect game 27 years earlier.

Born on the Fourth of July, Yankees owner George Steinbrenner liked nothing better than to see his team win. So the gift Steinbrenner received July 4, 1983, at Yankee Stadium proved to be especially meaningful for him and Yankees fans.

Throughout the early years of Steinbrenner's ownership of the Yankees, he was often personally involved in personnel decisions, from free agent acquisitions to trades. One such trade took place November 10, 1978, when the Yankees dealt five players and cash to the Texas Rangers for five players. Among the players acquired was left-hander Dave Righetti.

Righetti, who hailed from San Jose, California, had been the Rangers' number one pick in the 1977 January amateur draft and the 10th player chosen overall. While he showed a world of promise—his fastball could make even the most seasoned scout shake his head in admiration—he never seemed to be able to harness the elusive element of consistency. The Yankees called him to the show in 1979, and he compiled an 0-1 record with a 3.71 ERA in three starts. He didn't see the major leagues again until 1981, when he won American League Rookie of the Year honors after going 8-4 with a 2.06 ERA in 15 starts. In the 1981 American League Division Series, Righetti showed how good he could be by picking up two wins against the Milwaukee Brewers, with a Game 2 start and a Game 5 relief appearance.

Still, Righetti seemed to flirt with joining the upper echelon of major-league pitchers without quite ever reaching that lofty plateau. In 1982, Steinbrenner grew so frustrated with Righetti that he had him sent to Triple-A Columbus for three weeks.

A different Righetti showed up for the Yankees in 1983. And his arrival could not have come at a better time, given the fact that longtime staff ace Ron Guidry no longer resembled the "Louisiana Lightning" of previous years. At the ripe old age of 24, Righetti assumed the number one slot, and got busy compiling nine wins by the time he took to the mound at Yankee Stadium to face the Boston Red Sox on July 4, 1983.

Righetti faced a hot-hitting Red Sox team that had tallied nine home runs and scored 25 runs in the previous three games. Righetti joked with his teammates before the game that the Red Sox were in too good of a groove and that he would take care of business.

"I think I was just floating after the last out. The entire thing came as a blur to me. I only woke up after all my teammates began pounding me."

—Dave Righetti

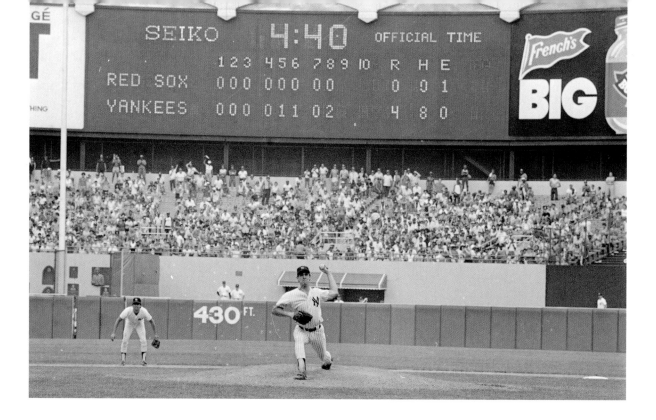

A portent for how well Righetti would pitch came in the first inning, when he struck out Jerry Remy, Wade Boggs, and Tony Armas. By the end of the third inning, he'd struck out seven.

Meanwhile, Righetti had a tight defense behind him. Bert Campaneris, the veteran infielder in his last season, made a saving play in the fourth. Armas hit a feeble two-out ground ball toward Campaneris, playing deep at third. Campaneris charged the ball, snapped his throw to rookie Don Mattingly, and managed to nip Armas at first. Yankees shortstop Roy Smalley then grabbed Glenn Hoffman's Texas leaguer while running with his back to the infield for the second out of the sixth. Thanks to Smalley, Righetti's chance at a no-hitter remained alive.

Righetti began to fight nervousness when he carried the no-hitter through eight innings. Almost two years had passed since Nolan Ryan had pitched the major league's last no-hitter; it had been two years since an American Leaguer had one. Righetti avoided looking at his teammates, but a calm finally came to him when he took a look around and saw that a Yankee Stadium crowd of 41,077 was going bonkers. He enjoyed the atmosphere.

Jeff Newman led off the Red Sox ninth and drew a walk. Hoffman then hit a two-strike pitch that could have been a double play, but ended up being a fielder's choice for the first out. Remy grounded out to second on the first pitch, leaving Righetti just one out from earning a spot among baseball's best pitchers.

But it wouldn't be easy. Stepping to the plate was none other than Wade Boggs. The Red Sox third baseman carried a .357 batting average, and he held claim to the fact he was one of the hardest hitters to strike out in the major leagues. The fans stood and roared.

The count went to 2-2 when catcher Butch Wynegar ran through the pitch selection. At first, he wanted Righetti to go with his best pitch, the fastball. But Wynegar instead decided to call a slider.

Righetti delivered the 132nd pitch of the game. Boggs swung and missed.

Righetti gleefully jumped in the air with his no-hitter intact. Yankee Stadium had not seen a no-hitter since Don Larsen had twirled a perfect game against the Brooklyn Dodgers in Game 5 of the 1956 World Series.

After the game, Righetti told reporters, "I was nervous, definitely, without a doubt. Everybody was nervous. They were making me nervous. I didn't look in the dugout because I didn't want to get more nervous. But I calmed down. I was enjoying the fans. I was enjoying being a Yankee."

"Normally when Rags pitched we expected him to do big things. More than anything I remember it was the Fourth of July. We had been to a concert the night before, Willie Nelson, a big concert at the Meadowlands, and then here it was, a hot day, and he just kept getting better and better."

—Don Mattingly

**Opposite Page:** Although "Rags" was not quite perfect during the game, allowing four walks, he overpowered the Red Sox early on. In the first three innings, he struck out seven.

Like Allie Reynolds against Ted Williams in 1951, Righetti had to retire a Red Sox immortal, Wade Boggs, to clinch his no-hitter. More than 41,000 fans roared their approval.

# From Ace to Closer

The Yankees used Dave Righetti as a starting pitcher during his first four seasons in the major leagues. His best season came in 1983, when he went 14-8 with a 3.44 ERA—including the memorable no-hitter. But in 1984, the Yankees needed a closer in their bullpen and, given Righetti's big fastball, he assumed the role and didn't miss a beat. In Righetti's first season as the team's closer, he compiled 31 saves and exceeded 20 saves eight times in his career. Righetti's high-water mark came in 1986, when he reached the top of his profession by leading the American League in saves with 46, breaking Bruce Sutter's major-league record. In doing so, Righetti earned the distinction as the first pitcher in major-league history to throw a no-hitter and also lead the league in saves.

## Pitchers Who Threw No-Hitters and Led League in Saves

Since 1969 when saves became an official statistic in the major leagues, only three pitchers have been credited with a complete-game no-hitter and led their league in saves.

| Pitchers | No-Hitter |
|---|---|
| Dave Righetti | July 14, 1983, for Yankees vs. Red Sox |
| | **Saves Leader** |
| | Led AL with 46 saves for Yankees in 1986 |
| Dennis Eckersley | **No-Hitter** |
| | May 30, 1977, for Indians vs. Angels |
| | **Saves Leader** |
| | Led AL in saves in 1988 (45) and 1991 (51) for A's |
| Derek Lowe | **No-Hitter** |
| | April 27, 2002, for Red Sox vs. Devil Rays |
| | **Saves Leader** |
| | Topped AL with 42 saves in 2000 for Red Sox |

31

# Abbott's Superhuman Feat

## September 4, 1993

A year before joining the Yankees, Jim Abbott won MLB's Tony Conigliaro Award for overcoming adversity through the attributes of spirit, determination, and courage.

**Opposite Page:** Kenny Lofton tried to bunt his way on in the ninth inning. Abbott had proven years earlier that he could handle bunted balls even though he didn't wear a mitt when he released the ball.

It was the Saturday of Labor Day weekend, and labor is what Yankees fans expected to do at the stadium that afternoon. George Steinbrenner's team hadn't made the playoffs in 12 years, and they were looking up at first-place Toronto in the AL East by two games. On this soggy, overcast day, the stadium was half-empty, and the 27,125 diehards had little faith in their starting pitcher.

Jim Abbott sported a 9-11 record with a 4.31 ERA. In his previous start, Cleveland had battered the hurler for seven runs, frustrating him so much that he punished himself with a three-mile run through the streets of Cleveland. Now facing the Indians again on September 4, Abbott walked Kenny Lofton to open the game. Sighs of frustration wafted through the stands. What do you expect, some must have muttered, from a one-handed pitcher?

Born without a right hand, Abbott had rocketed to fame, thanks to extraordinary perseverance and a golden left arm. A star for the University of Michigan and the 1988 U.S. Olympic Team, he joined the California Angels in 1989 without ever having played in the minors. He enjoyed his best season in 1991, when he went 18-11. In 1993, his first year in pinstripes, he hoped to pitch well down the stretch to salvage a disappointing season.

Abbott caught a break in the first inning, when he erased Lofton on a double-play ball. From there, his fortunes improved. He yielded only a walk in the second, and he recorded perfect frames in the third and fourth. He seemed more confident than in his previous start. "The real adjustment was mostly trusting my pitches a little more and getting ahead in the count," he said. Abbott jammed Cleveland's hitters with his cut fastball, which they repeatedly pounded into the soft turf. He recorded three groundouts in the fourth and a double-play grounder, following a walk, in the fifth. In the sixth, Jim Thome rifled a shot that shortstop Randy Velarde snared. After a walk, a fly-out, and a groundout, Abbott had completed two-thirds of the game without allowing a hit.

The crowd began to stir. Only six Yankees pitchers had ever pitched a no-hitter. And now here was Abbott, the one-handed marvel, just nine outs away from a fairy-tale performance. Catcher Matt Nokes, who had talked to Abbott in the dugout after every inning, now decided to clam up. In baseball, according to tradition, you don't talk to a pitcher who's throwing a no-hitter.

With one out in the seventh, third baseman Wade Boggs dove to his left to corral an Albert Belle grounder, then gunned him out. Boggs then handled an easy grounder to end the inning. The crowd went wild. "The fans were so into the game and the no-hitter that it was impossible to ignore what was going on," Abbott recalled. "Again it came back to focusing on the mitt and trusting the pitch—staying entirely in the moment and the process…. It felt like the calm in the middle of a storm."

With the Yankees up 4-0, Abbott opened the eighth by striking out Manny Ramirez and ended it with a groundout to third by Sandy Alomar. In the ninth, Abbott's biggest concern should have been his infielders. Velarde said he was so nervous, he could barely move his legs. First baseman Don Mattingly had "huge goosebumps on my forearms, and the hair on the back of my neck was standing up."

Leading off the inning, Lofton tried to bunt his way on, angering the crowd. When that didn't work, he grounded out to second. Felix Fermin followed with a 390-foot shot to left-center, but center fielder Bernie Williams chased it down on the warning track.

"I called Jim and congratulated him, and told him he probably doesn't realize the significance of pitching a no-hitter for the Yankees. It's still brought up to me all the time. It's amazing how many people can tell you where they were that day."

—Dave Righetti

With two outs, perennial .300 hitter Carlos Baerga stepped into the box. Baerga tapped a soft grounder to Velarde, who charged in for the ball and threw to first—in time! "The final out seemed to be in slow motion," Abbott recalled. "And then, bam, immediately back into fast forward." Abbott opened his arms wide and blared, "How about that, baby!"

Catcher Nokes ran to hug his pitcher, who was soon mobbed by his teammates. Abbott tipped his cap to the fans as he headed to the dugout, but they demanded a curtain call, which he granted. "I remember watching Baerga ground out to Velarde to end the game," said Yankees right fielder Paul O'Neill, "and the first thing that came to my mind was that Jim Abbott had one hand, and here he is with the Yankees throwing a no-hitter. It couldn't be more amazing."

Catcher Matt Nokes (wearing mitt) may have been the happiest man in the house after the no-hitter. When Abbott was struggling earlier in the year, Nokes had sat next to him between innings so they could analyze his pitching.

**Opposite Page:** Cleveland's Albert Belle blasted 38 homers with 129 RBI in 1993. He almost grounded a single to left in the seventh inning, but third baseman Wade Boggs saved the no-hitter with a diving stop and a strike to first.

"The last couple of innings, I had these huge goosebumps on my forearms, and the hair on the back of my neck was standing up. Maybe that would have happened with someone else. Maybe I'd have the same feelings. But I think because it was Jim, there was a little something extra."

—Don Mattingly

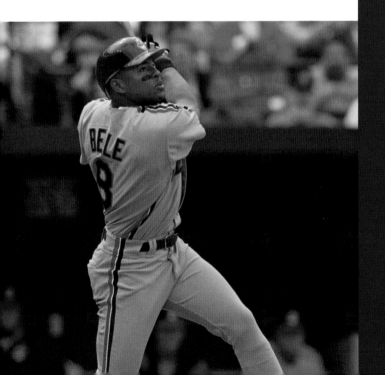

# Overachiever

Kids can be cruel, as Jim Abbott found out. As a child, he tried wearing a prosthesis, but he scrapped it after schoolmates called him "Mr. Hook." Moreover, his peers wouldn't let him play in pickup baseball games. Nevertheless, the strong-willed kid from Michigan was determined to succeed in sports. In his very first Little League baseball game, at age 11, Jim Abbott fired a no-hitter.

From then on, Abbott was king of the pitching hill. As a senior at Flint Central High School, he struck out 148 batters and allowed just 16 hits in 73 innings. He also batted .427 with seven home runs. He even starred as a quarterback on the varsity football team, throwing four touchdown passes in the state semifinal game.

As a pitcher for the University of Michigan, Abbott won the James E. Sullivan Award as the nation's best amateur athlete in 1987. He won a gold medal in the 1988 Olympics, and he joined the California Angels the following spring. After outstanding seasons in 1991 and '92 (ERAs of 2.89 and 2.77), he was shipped to the Yankees in a trade for J. T. Snow.

In his two seasons in New York, Abbott posted a mediocre 20-22 record. The city's children nonetheless looked up to Abbott, whose incredible story of overcoming adversity inspired them. In fact, he spent much of his free time visiting kids with disabilities.

After a disastrous 2-18 season with the Angels in 1996, Abbott retired, only to stage a successful comeback two years later. In five total starts with the Chicago White Sox in 1998, he went 5-0. Fittingly enough, Abbott now works as a motivational speaker.

# Still Plenty Good

## May 14, 1996

The Yankees hoist Gooden on their shoulders after his stunning no-hitter. The former Mets phenom had missed the entire previous season after being suspended for cocaine use.

**Opposite Page:** The man of the hour celebrates with catcher Joe Girardi. Though Gooden would make close to 100 more starts in his major-league career, this would be his last complete-game victory.

As a young man, Dwight Gooden owned New York City. During his rookie season of 1984, the 19-year-old Mets phenom led the National League in strikeouts. Along the way he acquired the nickname Dr. K, and Shea Stadium rocked every time he pitched. A Cy Young Award came next, and seven years into his career, Gooden's won-loss record stood at an incredible 119-46.

Unfortunately, Gooden also lived in the fast lane—that is, until he crashed and burned with an 18-month drug suspension from baseball. Arm problems further complicated things for Gooden, which made it easier for the Mets to part ways with him, once his suspension had been served. At the height of his well-publicized troubles, Gooden questioned whether he would ever play baseball again.

Enter George Steinbrenner.

The Yankees owner took interest in resurrecting Gooden's career and signed him prior to the 1996 season. But the Gooden that fans saw in Yankees pinstripes did not appear to be the same model who fashioned the pinstripes for the Mets.

Steinbrenner's good will gesture seemed destined to fail at the beginning. In Gooden's first three starts of the 1996 season, he surrendered 17 runs on 20 hits, while his ERA swelled to 11.48. He pitched better the next two starts, only he lacked stamina and didn't get far enough into the game to get a decision. His lackluster, early-season performances prompted whispers that the end of Gooden's illustrious career might be near. The Yankees relegated Gooden to the bullpen; there was even talk he would be shipped down to Triple-A Columbus.

Fortunately for Gooden, Mel Stottlemyre, his former pitching coach with the Mets, served in the same role with the Yankees. He tinkered with Gooden's mechanics, telling Gooden to take a shorter stride to the plate.

On May 8, Gooden put Stottlemyre's work on display and held the Tigers to two hits in eight innings, picking up his first win in almost two years. Catching everyone's attention was the fact that Gooden retired the final 22 Tigers hitters he faced.

Athletes deal with off-the-field problems just like everybody else. In addition to fighting a substance abuse problem, Gooden was consumed with worry about his father's ailing health. Kidney dialysis treatments three times a week had been a part of his father's life for the previous seven years.

Heading into his May 14 scheduled start against the Mariners, Gooden knew that his 68-year-old father would be having open-heart surgery the next day in Tampa, Florida. The Yankees left the decision of whether or not to pitch up to Gooden, who decided pitching was what his father wanted him to do. He figured he would make his start, then catch a flight to his hometown so he could be there when his father went into surgery.

Yankee Stadium hosted 31,025 fans for the Mariners-Yankees tilt, many of whom wondered whether Gooden had indeed rediscovered his Mets magic.

At the time when it happened, nobody thought much about the drive Seattle shortstop Alex Rodriguez greeted Gooden with in the first inning—the drive that center fielder Gerald Williams chased down. Williams started left, then went back right before stabbing the drive at the wall.

After Williams' first-inning help, Gooden took charge, effectively mixing his fastball with a curve to keep the Mariners' hitters off-balance. Suddenly, Gooden found himself pitching in the ninth inning, and the Mariners still did not have a hit. Could the resurrection of Dwight Gooden include a no-hitter? Such a thought was intoxicating to the fans, none of whom had left Yankee Stadium.

When he took the mound in the ninth inning, holding a 2-0 lead, Gooden received a standing ovation. He would now have to face the toughest part of the Mariners' order to achieve baseball immortality. The first three scheduled batters, Rodriguez, Ken Griffey Jr., and Edgar Martinez, would all hit over .300 that season.

Gooden walked Rodriguez to start the inning before Tino Martinez dove to tag first base and retire Griffey on a groundout. After walking Martinez on a 3-2 pitch, Gooden threw a wild pitch that allowed the runners to advance to second and third. But Gooden recovered to strike out Jay Buhner on a 2-2 fastball to bring up powerful Paul Sorrento, who would hit 23 home runs and drive in 93 runs that season. Sorrento popped up the fourth pitch, rookie shortstop Derek Jeter camped underneath it, and Gooden completed the improbable, evoking images of his former Mets' glory days. Gooden's teammates carried him

With two on and two out in the ninth, Gooden induced Paul Sorrento (pictured) to pop up. Rookie shortstop Derek Jeter caught the ball to complete the no-hitter.

Gooden improved dramatically in 1996 after shortening his stride to the plate. In his start prior to the no-hitter, Gooden surrendered two walks, two hits, one hit batsman, and three runs in the first inning before retiring the last 22 batters he faced.

from the field while the roar inside Yankee Stadium paid him homage.

As Gooden later said, "I think this is the greatest feeling, especially because I did it in New York. With all I've been through and all the stuff that has gone on, this is the greatest feeling."

In the aftermath of the no-hitter—which greatly pleased his father—Gooden arrived in Tampa early the next morning to be on hand when his father underwent successful double-bypass heart surgery.

**Dwight Gooden** was one of over 100 players to play for both the **Yankees and the Mets.**

| | | |
|---|---|---|
| Juan Acevedo | Lee Guetterman | Hal Reniff |
| Jack Aker | Greg A. Harris | Kenny Rogers |
| Neil Allen | Rickey Henderson | Rey Sanchez |
| Sandy Alomar Sr. | Felix Heredia | Rafael Santana |
| Jason Anderson | Orlando Hernandez | Don Schulze |
| Tucker Ashford | Keith Hughes | Bill Short |
| Armando Benitez | Stan Jefferson | Charley Smith |
| Yogi Berra | Lance Johnson | Shane Spencer |
| Daryl Boston | Dave Kingman | Roy Staiger |
| Darren Bragg | Matt Lawton | Mike Stanton |
| Tim Burke | Tim Leary | Kelly Stinnett |
| Ray Burris | Ricky Ledee | Darryl Strawberry |
| Miguel Cairo | Al Leiter | Tom Sturdivant |
| John Candelaria | Cory Lidle | Bill Sudakis |
| Duke Carmel | Phil Linz | Ron Swoboda |
| Alberto Castillo | Graeme Lloyd | Frank Tanana |
| Rick Cerone | Phil Lombardi | Tony Tarasco |
| Tony Clark | Terrence Long | Walt Terrell |
| David Cone | Bob MacDonald | Ralph Terry |
| Billy Cowan | Elliott Maddox | Ryan Thompson |
| Wilson Delgado | Josias Manzanillo | Marv Throneberry |
| Octavio Dotel | Lee Mazzilli | Dick Tidrow |
| Dock Ellis | Doc Medich | Mike Torrez |
| Kevin Elster | Doug Mientkiewicz | Bubba Trammell |
| Scott Erickson | Dale Murray | Robin Ventura |
| Alvaro Espinoza | C. J. Nitkowski | Jose Vizcaino |
| Tony Fernandez | Bob Ojeda | Claudell Washington |
| Tim Foli | John Olerud | Allen Watson |
| Bob Friend | Jesse Orosco | Dave Weathers |
| Karim Garcia | John Pacella | Wally Whitehurst |
| Rob Gardner | Juan Padilla | Gerald Williams |
| Paul Gibson | Lenny Randle | Gene Woodling |
| Jesse Gonder | Willie Randolph | Todd Zeile |
| Dwight Gooden | Jeff Reardon | |

# What Happened?  Perfection!

## May 17, 1998

Wells was razor sharp with his control, not just against the Twins on May 17 but throughout the rest of the season as well. He allowed just 1.22 walks per nine innings, by far the best mark in the league.

**Opposite Page:** Three Yankees (Bernie Williams, Willie Banks, and Darryl Strawberry, left to right) are needed to carry Boomer off the field. Wells answered critics who said he was too heavy to pitch effectively.

The Yankees clubhouse was abuzz when comedian Billy Crystal made his way toward pitcher David Wells. "I got here late," Crystal quipped. "What happened?"

What happened was laced with so many amazing ironies and bizarre coincidences that it could only have happened to … well, David Wells. Just days earlier, Wells had contemplated retirement. In Texas on May 6, the Yankees had provided him with a 9-0 lead, but he couldn't pitch his way out of the third inning. Frustrated upon his exit, he flipped the ball disrespectfully to manager Joe Torre. Afterward, he reportedly talked about hanging up his spikes for good.

In his next start, however, Wells beat the Royals. Buoyed by that victory, he brushed off the humiliating Texas defeat, saying, "I just go out and do my job. If I'm successful, great; if not I've got to bounce back. It's just one of those things. Quality players can bounce back and don't give up. If you look at my track record, I've always been a fighter."

Wells entered the Twins game just three days shy of his 35th birthday. His 5.23 ERA was as hefty as his physique. Like ballplayers of earlier eras, Wells, nicknamed "Boomer," lived and partied hard, and he looked it. One of baseball's most notorious bad boys, Wells pierced his ear and tattooed his body. He hung out with the Hell's Angels and boasted of his beer drinking. In fact, just a year earlier, he had broken his hand during an ugly bar fight. He would later write a book entitled *Perfect I'm Not: Boomer on Beer, Brawls, Backaches, and Baseball*. For the cover photo, he leaned on a motorcycle while sporting a white tank top.

Wells seemed to revel in proving that an out-of-shape hurler like himself could thrive in the big leagues. However, Torre felt that his potbellied pitcher was tempting fate. After the Texas game, the straitlaced skipper stated that Wells' excessive weight (245 pounds!) was affecting his pitching, and held a closed-door meeting with Wells and pitching coach Mel Stottlemyre. Nevertheless, Wells had many supporters—especially among the bleacher-bum section. Some claimed that Boomer was in the mold of Babe Ruth, who lived largely on a diet of hot dogs and beer. Wells, who grew up a Yankees fan, knew all about the Babe's exploits. Like Ruth, Wells was an effective lefty pitcher, having won 16 games in both 1995

(10 with Detroit and 6 for Cincinnati) and '97 (Yankees). Wells even owned an original Ruth cap, which he once tried to wear during a Yankees game until the umpires told him to take it off.

When Boomer took the hill on May 17, he was nursing a hangover after attending a *Saturday Night Live* cast party. He may have thought that he was in for a long day, but with his whistling fastball and sharp-breaking curveball, Wells set down the Twins in order through the first three innings. He went to 3-0 on Matt Lawton in the fourth, but he retired him as well. Through seven frames, he remained perfect, with no Twin even coming close to getting a hit. New York held a comfortable 4-0 lead.

"One thing I spent a lot of time talking to David about was doing more to finish off hitters when he was ahead in the count. That day against the Twins he did that great. As the game went on, I stayed away from David because there wasn't anything I could really tell him. Plus I didn't want to mess with his karma."

—Mel Stottlemyre

Wells liked to commiserate with his teammates, including pitcher Hideki Irabu (pictured). During the perfect game, only David Cone dared to break tradition and chat with the fellow hurler.

**Opposite Page:** For a perfect game, Wells threw a lot of pitches—120. He fired 79 strikes and 41 balls, and he struck out 11 batters.

In the Yankees dugout, as per baseball tradition, no one would talk to Wells. Only fellow pitcher David Cone (who would toss his own perfecto a year later) dared to break the silence, jokingly telling Wells to start throwing the knuckleball.

In the eighth, Ron Coomer nearly shattered the no-hitter. Second baseman Chuck Knoblauch initially couldn't handle his hard grounder, but he recovered to throw Coomer out. When Wells returned to the dugout, Cone chided him, "You showed me nothing out there, you wimp."

In the top of the ninth, in the late-afternoon shadows, 49,820 fans thundered their support for Boomer. "I was hoping the fans would kind of shush a little bit," Wells said. "They were making me nervous." In fact, like Don Larsen in his perfect game in 1956, Wells's body was turning to jelly. "By the end," Wells said, "I could barely grip the ball, my hand was shaking so much."

Nevertheless, the portly portsider cruised in the ninth. Jon Shave flew out meekly to right fielder Paul O'Neill, and Javier Valentin struck out—Wells' 11th of the game. Finally, Pat Meares lofted another easy fly ball that O'Neill corralled.

Amid the crowd's roar, Wells fell to his knees and pumped his fist twice. His teammates rushed to the mound and hoisted him on their shoulders, as the PA system blared "New York, New York" by Frank Sinatra, who had died three days earlier. In the clubhouse, Boomer took a call from Larsen, who—incredibly enough—had attended the same San Diego high school as Wells.

Over the next three days, Wells celebrated in Ruthian fashion. He partied with friends on Sunday night, did *The Late Show with David Letterman* on Monday, and received the Key to the City from New York Mayor Rudy Giuliani on Tuesday—while dressed in a pair of jeans.

"Wells was a good-time guy, and I had my fun, too. Also a coincidence we both went to the same high school in San Diego. When I congratulated him, I told him he won't forget pitching a perfect game. He'll think about it almost every day, like I do."

—Don Larsen

# 27 Up, 27 Down

## MINNESOTA

|  | AB | R | H | RBI |
|---|---|---|---|---|
| Matt Lawton, cf | 3 | 0 | 0 | 0 |
| Brent Gates, 2b | 3 | 0 | 0 | 0 |
| Paul Molitor, dh | 3 | 0 | 0 | 0 |
| Marty Cordova, lf | 3 | 0 | 0 | 0 |
| Ron Coomer, 1b | 3 | 0 | 0 | 0 |
| Alex Ochoa, rf | 3 | 0 | 0 | 0 |
| Jon Shave, 3b | 3 | 0 | 0 | 0 |
| Javier Valentin, c | 3 | 0 | 0 | 0 |
| Pat Meares, ss | 3 | 0 | 0 | 0 |
| TOTALS | 27 | 0 | 0 | 0 |

## NEW YORK

|  | AB | R | H | RBI |
|---|---|---|---|---|
| Chuck Knoblauch, 2b | 4 | 0 | 0 | 0 |
| Derek Jeter, ss | 3 | 0 | 1 | 0 |
| Paul O'Neill, rf | 4 | 0 | 0 | 0 |
| Tino Martinez, 1b | 4 | 0 | 0 | 0 |
| Bernie Williams, cf | 3 | 3 | 3 | 1 |
| Darryl Strawberry, dh | 3 | 1 | 1 | 1 |
| Chad Curtis, lf | 3 | 0 | 1 | 1 |
| Jorge Posada, c | 3 | 0 | 0 | 0 |
| Scott Brosius, 3b | 3 | 0 | 0 | 0 |
| TOTALS | 30 | 4 | 6 | 3 |

Doubles: Williams 2
Triples: Strawberry
Home runs: Williams
Left on base: New York 3
Stolen bases: Jeter, Curtis

## MINNESOTA

|  | IP | H | R | ER | BB | SO |
|---|---|---|---|---|---|---|
| LaTroy Hawkins | 7.0 | 6 | 4 | 4 | 0 | 5 |
| Dan Naulty | 0.1 | 0 | 0 | 0 | 1 | 0 |
| Greg Swindell | 0.2 | 0 | 0 | 0 | 0 | 1 |

## NEW YORK

|  | IP | H | R | ER | BB | SO |
|---|---|---|---|---|---|---|
| David Wells | 9.0 | 0 | 0 | 0 | 0 | 11 |

Winning pitcher: Wells (5-1)
Losing pitcher: Hawkins (2-4)

|  | 1 | 2 | 3 | 4 | 5 | 6 | 7 | 8 | 9 | R | H | E |
|---|---|---|---|---|---|---|---|---|---|---|---|---|
| Minnesota | 0 | 0 | 0 | 0 | 0 | 0 | 0 | 0 | 0 | 0 | 0 | 0 |
| New York | 0 | 1 | 0 | 1 | 0 | 0 | 2 | 0 | x | 4 | 6 | 0 |

Attendance: 49,820
Time of game: 2:40

# Cone Replicates Perfecto

## July 18, 1999

Davide Cone employed a nasty slider to silence the Montreal bats. He threw just 88 pitches, 68 of which were strikes.

**Opposite Page:** Catcher Joe Girardi and second baseman Chuck Knoblauch hoist Cone on their shoulders. The southpaw weathered a rain delay and 95-degree heat en route to nine perfect innings.

A crowd of 41,930 fans marched eagerly into Yankee Stadium on July 18, 1999, before a game between the Yankees and the Montreal Expos. They had come to the Bronx for Yogi Berra Day to welcome a returning hero. Having been fired as manager in 1985, and then vowing never to enter Yankee Stadium while George Steinbrenner owned the team, Berra had settled his differences with Steinbrenner. After 14 years of self-imposed exile, the franchise's most beloved catcher was finally coming back to the stadium for a long overdue tribute.

The day was supposed to belong to Berra, who had helped the Yankees win 10 World Series championships. Several old-timers, including Whitey Ford, Phil Rizzuto, Gil McDougald, and Bobby Richardson, had come to the venerable ballpark to honor him in a 30-minute, pregame ceremony. Then Don Larsen threw out the ceremonial first pitch to Berra, who had been Larsen's battery mate in the only World Series perfect game, in 1956.

Pitching for the Yankees that day was David Cone, a right-hander with more deliveries than Jay Leno. After Larsen completed his toss, he and Cone shook hands near the mound. Cone jokingly asked if Larsen was going to jump into Berra's arms like he did in 1956. According to Cone, Larsen replied, "Kid, you got it wrong. It was Yogi jumped into my arms."

It would be the only mistake Cone made that afternoon. He retired the side in order in the first and second innings. After a 33-minute rain delay, he struck out the side in the third inning, and whizzed through a 1-2-3 fourth. By the sixth inning, the fans at Yankee Stadium were reveling in every pitch, and when Rondell White struck out to end the seventh, the crowd's roar lingered long after Cone had disappeared into the dugout.

The fans in Yankee Stadium were buzzing. Only six outs to go, and Cone would accomplish the unthinkable by pitching a perfect game. Brad Fullmer whiffed for out number 24. Three outs away. In the ninth, Cone fanned Chris Widger for the first out. Ryan McGuire pinch-hit for Shane Andrews and looped a ball that left fielder Ricky Ledee caught on the run. One out to go. When Orlando Cabrera popped to third baseman Scott Brosius for the

"Being there as part of Yogi Berra Day, that made it really special. It was exciting to watch and I'm sure Yogi was also thinking this may be déjà vu all over again, like he says. I was very happy for David. And I was glad I finally got a chance to see one. I never saw mine."

—Don Larsen

final out, Cone dropped to his knees and grabbed his head in disbelief, like Bjorn Borg when he won his fifth consecutive Wimbledon singles title in 1980.

After being carried off the field by his teammates, Cone told reporters, "I probably have a better chance of winning the lottery than this happening today. It makes you stop and think about the Yankee magic and the mystique of this ballpark." He retired all 27 Montreal batters he faced as the Yankees defeated the Expos 6-0. It was only the 16th perfect game in modern major-league baseball history, and yet the third at Yankee Stadium. Of the previous 15 perfect games, Cone's was perhaps the most efficient. He threw only 88 pitches and didn't go to a three-ball count on a single batter. Working in stifling 95-degree heat, Cone was coolly in command, using a wicked slider to strike out 10 and induce 13 fly-outs and four grounders.

Cone falls to his knees as catcher Joe Girardi rushes to greet him.

**Opposite Page:** Don Larsen, on hand for Yogi Berra Day, congratulates Cone. They now shared a special kinship: Yankees pitchers who had authored perfect games.

His premier performance was all the more remarkable because of his age—at 36, he was the oldest pitcher to throw a perfect game since Cy Young in 1904—and the career-threatening surgery he had endured three seasons earlier to treat an aneurysm in his pitching arm.

Cone, who pitched three career one-hitters, said he wondered if he'd ever get a chance at a no-hitter again. "Going into the latter innings today, running through my mind [was] how many times I've been close and how this might be the last chance I get," he told *The New York Times*. "My heart was pumping. I could feel it through my uniform."

One man in the stands could identify with what Cone was feeling.

"I was just thinking about my day," Larsen told Peter Schmuck of *The Sporting News*. "I'm sure David will think about this every day of his life."

"It was a heck of a day, it really was. To be honored with all my family there, that was great, then catching the [ceremonial] first pitch from Don. Watching Cone pitch like he did brought back memories you won't forget. Me and Don gave him a big hug in the clubhouse—just a great day."

—Yogi Berra

# How David Did It

**MONTREAL**

|  | AB | R | H | RBI |
|---|---|---|---|---|
| Wilton Guerrero, dh | 3 | 0 | 0 | 0 |
| Terry Jones, cf | 2 | 0 | 0 | 0 |
| James Mouton, cf | 1 | 0 | 0 | 0 |
| Rondell White, lf | 3 | 0 | 0 | 0 |
| Vladimir Guerrero, rf | 3 | 0 | 0 | 0 |
| Jose Vidro, 2b | 3 | 0 | 0 | 0 |
| Brad Fullmer, 1b | 3 | 0 | 0 | 0 |
| Chris Widger, c | 3 | 0 | 0 | 0 |
| Shane Andrews, 3b | 2 | 0 | 0 | 0 |
| Ryan McGuire, ph | 1 | 0 | 0 | 0 |
| Orlando Cabrera, ss | 3 | 0 | 0 | 0 |
| TOTALS | 27 | 0 | 0 | 0 |

**NEW YORK**

|  | AB | R | H | RBI |
|---|---|---|---|---|
| Chuck Knoblauch, 2b | 2 | 1 | 1 | 0 |
| Derek Jeter, ss | 4 | 1 | 1 | 2 |
| Paul O'Neill, rf | 4 | 1 | 1 | 0 |
| Bernie Williams, cf | 4 | 0 | 1 | 1 |
| Tino Martinez, 1b | 4 | 0 | 1 | 0 |
| Chili Davis, dh | 3 | 1 | 1 | 0 |
| Ricky Ledee, lf | 4 | 1 | 1 | 2 |
| Scott Brosius, 3b | 2 | 1 | 0 | 0 |
| Joe Girardi, c | 3 | 0 | 1 | 1 |
| TOTALS | 30 | 6 | 8 | 6 |

Doubles: Girardi, O'Neill
Home runs: Ledee, Jeter
Left on base: New York 3

**MONTREAL**

|  | IP | H | R | ER | BB | SO |
|---|---|---|---|---|---|---|
| Javier Vazquez | 7.2 | 7 | 6 | 6 | 2 | 3 |
| Bobby Ayala | 1.1 | 1 | 0 | 0 | 0 | 0 |

**NEW YORK**

|  | IP | H | R | ER | BB | SO |
|---|---|---|---|---|---|---|
| David Cone | 9.0 | 0 | 0 | 0 | 0 | 10 |

Winning Pitcher: Cone (10-4)
Losing Pitcher: Vazquez (2-5)

|  | 1 | 2 | 3 | 4 | 5 | 6 | 7 | 8 | 9 | R | H | E |
|---|---|---|---|---|---|---|---|---|---|---|---|---|
| Montreal | 0 | 0 | 0 | 0 | 0 | 0 | 0 | 0 | 0 | 0 | 0 | 0 |
| New York | 0 | 5 | 0 | 0 | 0 | 0 | 0 | 1 | x | 6 | 8 | 0 |

Attendance: 41,930
Time of Game: 2:16

# 400 and Counting

July 16, 2006

Rivera gets a hug from first-base coach Tony Pena after recording his 400th career save on July 16, 2006. He is the first closer with 400 or more lifetime saves to register all his saves with one team.

**Opposite Page:** Rivera has become renowned for his cool under pressure, pinpoint control, and cut fastball. His mid-90s cutter features a sharp, late break–often over the black of the plate.

A flicker of despair ran through the grandstand, as 54,781 fans nervously inched forward in their seats. The Yankees were clinging to a slim 6-4 lead against the Chicago White Sox at Yankee Stadium. In the eighth inning, Chicago had put two men on base with nobody out. Into these woeful circumstances entered Mariano Rivera, a reedy, right-handed relief pitcher from Panama with a steely focus and a sense of mental calm so great, he could sleep through a thunderstorm.

If there is one relief pitcher in the last decade who might personify the word *closer*, a stadium full of baseball experts might pick Rivera. Few, if any, relief pitchers enjoy the immense reputation that Rivera has earned with the Yankees. As team captain Derek Jeter says, "When he comes in the game, the mind-set is, it's over."

The game against Chicago was a typical Rivera appearance. The 36-year-old reliever tossed two innings of shutout ball, allowing one hit and one walk, and striking out one, to record the 400th regular-season save of his career. As a result, Rivera became the first reliever to save 400 games for one team. "To do it in New York, there's nothing better than that," said Rivera.

The vision of Rivera bursting through the bullpen door is enough to give even the most accomplished opposing hitters serious pause. With the Yankee Stadium sound system blaring Metallica's "Enter Sandman," and the fans raucously cheering in anticipation, he jogs across the outfield grass, strides gracefully to the mound, fires seven or eight warm-up pitches, stares blankly at his target with sharklike eyes, and then gets down to serious business.

"The song starts playing, the game's over," says Jason Giambi. Despite the perilous situation and the swelling crowd noise, whether for him or against him, any time Rivera arrives for his rescue act, he resists the pressure simply by ignoring it. Occasionally, he isn't even aware of the identity of the man swinging the bat at home plate. In manager Joe Torre's opinion, he has the ideal temperament for a closer.

"He's the best I've ever been around. Not only the ability to pitch and perform under pressure, but the calm he puts over the clubhouse."

Rivera doesn't quarrel with that view. "I don't get nervous. I trust God. If I get nervous, I can't do my job."

More than anyone else, it was Rivera doing his job that propelled the Yankees into World Series champions for three consecutive seasons, as he was on the mound to record the final out in each of the three clinching games in 1998, 1999, and 2000. October after October, the 6-foot-2, 185-pounder held precarious leads the Yankees had scratched together. He literally attacked rival hitters with one pitch: an unsolvable cut fastball that Torre has called a combination of thunder and location. Rivera's impact couldn't possibly be any greater. His lifetime postseason earned-run average of 0.77 (through 2007) is the major-league record. More impressive still, his record 34 postseason saves are more than twice that of his next closest competitor, Dennis Eckersley,

"Mo has such great athleticism and toughness. But he became more durable than anyone could've ever imagined. He was our set-up man, but made the transition to closer real easily when [John] Wetteland left after '96."

—Mel Stottlemyre

"To me the most amazing thing is Mo's demeanor; not too many people have what he has. He's never intimidated, he'll challenge anyone, and you can't tell from his expression whether he was successful the night before or failed the night before."

—Derek Jeter

**Opposite Page:** Rivera and Co. celebrate the Yankees' four-game sweep over Atlanta in the last major-league game ever played in the 20th century. Mariano logged two saves and a win to earn World Series MVP honors.

Manager Joe Torre had complete faith in Rivera, especially during the postseason. Through 2007, Mariano had gone 8-1 with 34 saves and a 0.77 ERA in 76 postseason games.

which explains why Rivera's teammates act as if they are about to inherit the family trust fund.

"Our whole game plan is to get a lead and give the ball to him in the ninth inning," said Paul O'Neill.

Final inventory figures for his career will show that all other relief pitchers will be shooting at his marks for a long time to come. But Mariano Rivera's contributions go beyond mere numbers, impressive as the numbers happen to be. It's the form as well as the substance that makes Rivera a star in the grand old Yankee tradition: humble, gracious, poised, and commanding. The fact that he's also a spiritual and faithful man makes him all the more valuable as an inspiration to his teammates and his opponents.

"On the field and off the field, he's a Hall of Famer," said Chicago White Sox manager Ozzie Guillen. "Young people should look up to him. He's the perfect player. God bless Joe Torre's Mariano." To Yankees fans, Guillen is preaching to the choir.

## Yankees' All-Time Save Leaders

| | | |
|---|---|---|
| 1. | Mariano Rivera | 443 |
| 2. | Dave Righetti | 224 |
| 3. | Rich Gossage | 151 |
| 4. | Sparky Lyle | 141 |
| 5. | Johnny Murphy | 104 |
| 6. | Steve Farr | 78 |
| 7. | Joe Page | 76 |
| 8. | John Wetteland | 74 |
| 9. | Lindy McDaniel | 58 |
| 10. | Luis Arroyo | 43 |
| | Ryne Duren | 43 |

Part 2

# October Classics

# A Wild Finish

## October 8, 1927

Earle Combs, who cracked 231 hits and scored 137 runs in 1927, scored the winning run in the Game 4 Series finale. He walked, was bunted over, and scored thanks to two wild pitches.

**Opposite Page:** Lou Gehrig (shown rounding third) electrified the home crowd in the first inning of Game 3 of the World Series. He tripled in two runs and was thrown out while trying for an inside-the-park home run. New York won 8-1.

A coronation took place at Yankee Stadium for a team history has judged as baseball royalty. But the crowning ceremony for the 1927 Yankees happened only after an exciting finish.

The mere mention of the '27 Yankees inspired fear in opponents. Even their nickname was ominous: Murderer's Row. Over the years, the team had defined what it meant to be a powerhouse. Few times in the history of baseball had a team been so well constructed with power, fielding, and pitching. And the results were predictable as the 1927 Yankees stormed to the American League pennant.

Babe Ruth led the Yankees with 60 home runs, a .356 batting average, and 164 RBI. Nicely complementing the greatest player of all time were Lou Gehrig, Earle Combs, Tony Lazzeri, and Bob Meusel.

Waite Hoyt's 22-7 mark led a staff that included Wilcy Moore, Herb Pennock, and Urban Shocker. Given the team's level of talent, the Yankees entered the World Series as heavy favorites to sweep the Pittsburgh Pirates in four games.

As for the Pirates, their star players were the outfield brothers, Paul and Lloyd Waner, nicknamed "Big Poison" and "Little Poison," respectively, due to their immense batting skills.

The Series opened at Pittsburgh's Forbes Field. The day before, the Pirates had made the grave mistake of watching the Yankees take batting practice. Indeed, seeing the entire Yankees lineup pepper all corners of Forbes Field only exacerbated the Pirates' worries about taking on the legendary Murderer's Row.

The Yankees took Game 1 5-4, with Hoyt picking up the win. Games 2 and 3 also went the Yankees' way by scores of 6-2 and 8-1, respectively, setting the table for the Yankees to complete the sweep in Game 4 at Yankee Stadium.

Prior to Game 3, floral arrangements in the shapes of horseshoes and baseball bats were given to Gehrig and Ruth. Once the game was complete, Yankees players returned to the clubhouse in the bowels of Yankee Stadium and playfully danced around the flowers, making

> "They always say the 1927 Yankees were the greatest team in the history of baseball. When you have four Hall of Famers in your lineup, including Ruth and Gehrig, well, I guess it'd be hard to argue."
>
> —Bobby Richardson

for a scene some might have observed to be a premature celebration. But they had plenty to celebrate. Pennock had held the Pirates scoreless through seven innings—before the Yankees put six runs on the board in the bottom of the seventh to take an 8-0 lead.

Game 4 at Yankee Stadium drew 57,909 fans, who watched Moore, starting for the Yankees, give up a leadoff single to Lloyd Waner in the first; he then scored on a Glenn Wright single to put the Pirates up 1-0. The Yankees answered against Pirates starter Carmen Hill in the bottom of the first, when Ruth's single to right field scored Combs.

Both pitchers seemed to settle into a rhythm until Hill had to face Ruth for the third time. Combs singled to lead off the fifth; after Mark Koenig struck out, the Sultan of Swat stepped up to the plate. Ruth connected, sending a towering drive into the right-field stands to put the Yankees up 3-1. Twelve outs separated the Yankees from another world championship. But the Pirates tallied two runs in the seventh to tie the score, thanks to errors by Moore and Lazzeri.

Johnny Miljus, "The Big Serb," came on in relief for the Pirates in the bottom of the seventh. He kept the Yankees off the scoreboard in his first two innings, while Moore continued to hold the Pirates in check. The score remained tied when the game moved into the bottom of the ninth.

It was raining lightly, and Miljus' magic seemed to be slipping away, when Combs walked on four pitches leading off the ninth. Koenig then beat out a bunt down the third-base line to put runners at first and second with no outs, and Ruth stepping to the plate.

Miljus cut loose with a wild pitch to advance the runners to second and third, which translated to an intentional walk for Ruth. After ball four, Ruth paused to talk briefly to Gehrig, then moved on to first base to load the bases.

Yankee Stadium had come to life. Yankees fans wanted Gehrig to end the game right then. He didn't. Miljus struck out the Iron Horse to bring Meusel to the plate. And once again, Miljus rose to the occasion by striking out the right-handed slugger for the second out.

With two outs and the prospect of the Pirates escaping to extra innings, Lazzeri stepped into the batter's box. Miljus got strike one on the Yankees second baseman, as drizzle continued to dampen the field.

The Pirates right-hander then uncorked a pitch that catcher John Gooch jumped for but failed to grab, as Combs raced home with the winning run to complete the four-game sweep.

The Yankees gave 60,000 fans their money's worth in the third game of the Series. Herb Pennock allowed one run on three hits, the Babe belted a homer, and the Yankees cruised 8-1.

**Opposite Page:** Manager Miller Huggins may have stood just 5'6", but he had plenty of big boys around him. Ruth and Gehrig drove in a combined 339 runs, and the Yankees scored 975 runs—130 more than any other AL team.

"I know that team dominated baseball like nobody else. It's hard to compare teams from different eras, but our '61 team also had it all—power, defense, pitching. We broke a heck of a lot of records, too."

—Johnny Blanchard

# $1.10 for World Series Tix

In order to attend the 1927 World Series, fans had to make reservations by mail through the Yankees' offices. Instructions on how to order tickets to the Series appeared in the September 17, 1927, edition of *The New York Times*. Reserved and box seats were to be sold in sets of three for Games 3, 4, and 5. In addition, 15,000 general admission and 20,000 bleacher tickets would be placed on sale the morning of each game. Ticket prices were $6.60 for box seats, $5.50 for reserved seats, $3.30 for general admission, and $1.10 for bleachers. Since the Yankees swept the Series, fans received refunds for the canceled Game 5.

The 1927 World Series was the fifth of the decade for the Yankees. Their first three appearances ever came in 1921-23 during the "Subway Series." The New York Giants won the first two of those fall classics before the Yankees got revenge in 1923.

The Yankees played the 1921 and '22 World Series at the Polo Grounds, which they and the Giants shared at the time. In 1923, the Yankees played in front of their first gargantuan Series crowds, drawing more than 62,000 in Games 3 and 5, at home, before clinching the world title on the road.

In the 1926 Series against St. Louis, more than 60,000 flocked to the first two games in New York, but only 38,093 showed up to see the Bombers lose Game 7 at Yankee Stadium. In 1927, 60,695 witnessed Game 3 in New York, and 57,909 bought tickets for the historic Game 4. It was the first time the Bombers ever clinched the World Series in the House That Ruth Built.

# The First Three-peat

## October 9, 1938

Bill Dickey, Lou Gehrig, Joe DiMaggio, and Tony Lazzeri (left to right) powered the 1936 Yankees, who scored an astounding 1,065 runs. Each of these men amassed more than 100 RBI, as did teammate George Selkirk.

**Opposite Page:** Shortstop Frank Crosetti slides in safely with a two-run triple in the second inning of the fourth game of the 1938 World Series. Crosetti plated four runners in the 8-3 game to help New York clinch the Series.

After the Yankees beat the Chicago Cubs in Game 2 of the 1938 World Series, Lou Gehrig sat quietly in the corner of the visitor's clubhouse at Wrigley Field. While his teammates celebrated, the Iron Horse propped his feet on a chair and puffed away at a cigarette. "I'm just sitting over here, seeing everything, hearing everything, and enjoying it all," he said.

Apparently, Gehrig had simply grown accustomed to Yankees success. He already had won 25 World Series games and five world championships. Moreover, in recent years, general manager Ed Barrow and manager Joe McCarthy had constructed the most powerful Yankees juggernaut yet. The Bombers had cruised to the world title in 1936 and '37 and were gunning for their third straight championship in '38—a feat no big-league team had ever accomplished.

The offense erupted in 1936 with the arrival of rookie Joe DiMaggio, who knocked in 125 runs. A year later, he belted .346 with 46 four-baggers. Gehrig amassed 311 RBI in 1936-37, and catcher Bill Dickey hit .362 in '36. Third baseman Red Rolfe and outfielder George Selkirk were perennial .300 hitters. On the hill, Red Ruffing won 20 games in each of the three seasons.

From 1936 through '38, the Yankees led the American League in runs and ERA every season, while winning the pennant by an average of 14 games. Over three games on May 23-24, 1936, the Yankees outscored the Philadelphia A's 52-9, including a 25-2 drubbing in the third contest.

The press derided McCarthy as a "push-button manager," one who filled out the same lineup card every day and then sat back and watched. But "Marse Joe" had complete control of this outfit. During road trips, all players had to arrive at breakfast at 8:30 sharp—in jackets and ties. McCarthy juggled his pitchers expertly. He also was an alert field general and a marvelous teacher. As DiMaggio said, "Never a day went by when you didn't learn something from McCarthy."

The Yankees opened 1938 concerned about Gehrig, who had seemingly lost his ability to drive the ball. As James M. Kahn wrote in the *New York Sun*, "He is meeting the ball

"Growing up in Astoria, I was a real Gehrig and DiMaggio
fan. I thought I was a decent hitter myself as a kid.
But in high school I became a pitcher and remember
watching Red Ruffing, who was the best. Great fastball,
wicked curve. And the best-hitting pitcher I ever saw."

—Whitey Ford

**Top:** After drawing a walk, Lou Gehrig scores the first run of the 1938 World Series, at Chicago's Wrigley Field. The "Iron Horse," who mustered just four singles in the Series, was in the early stages of ALS.

Red Ruffing was the ace of the 1936-39 dynasty, winning 20, 20, 21, and 21 games over the stretch. In the 1937-39 World Series, he went 4-0 in four complete-game starts, allowing a total of just five earned runs.

time after time, and it isn't going anywhere." However, Gehrig rebounded to bat .295-29-114—his worst season in 12 years, but enough to appease the worrywarts. Meanwhile, DiMaggio, Dickey, Rolfe, Joe Gordon, and Tommy Henrich combined to average 105 RBI. New York outscored its opponents 966-710 and finished 99-53—9½ games ahead of the second-place Red Sox.

The Cubs, who had been swept and humiliated by the Yankees in the 1932 World Series, were given no chance in the 1938 fall classic. Chicago had gone on a late-season tear to edge Pittsburgh for the NL pennant, but it still won only 89 games. Augie Galan led the team with just 69 RBI, and Ripper Collins paced the club with a mere 13 home runs.

In the Series opener at Wrigley Field, the Yankees cruised 3-1, thanks to the reliable Ruffing. Though Chicago led 3-2 in Game 2 behind sore-armed, soft-tossing Dizzy Dean, Crosetti and DiMaggio went deep in the eighth and ninth, respectively, to give New York a 6-3 victory. The teams hopped the train for the Big Apple, where the only worried Yankees fans were those who had tickets for Game 5.

In Game 3, in front of 55,236 fans, Monte "Hoot" Pearson breezed to a 5-2 complete-game victory, with Gordon knocking in three. For the third straight game, New York finished off the Cubs in less than two hours. And while Chicago hung tough in Game 4, trailing 4-3 in the eighth, the Yankees finished them off with four runs in the bottom of the frame—two coming on a bases-loaded bloop double by Crosetti. Ruffing closed down the Cubs in the ninth, personally tossing out Billy Herman to end it, for his second complete-game victory. Nearly 60,000 fans celebrated the first "three-peat" in major-league history.

In the raucous Yankees clubhouse, players burst into the songs "It's the Best Team in the Land" and "For He's a Jolly Good Fellow," while battery mates Ruffing and Dickey kissed for photographers. "We are the greatest ball club ever assembled, I firmly believe," McCarthy boasted. "We had everything and outclassed the Cubs at every turn."

Curiously, Gehrig stayed on the fringes of the celebration, smiling, sitting, and puffing another cigarette. He had batted .286 for the Series, but all four of his hits were singles. Something about him was just not right. The Yankees would cruise to a fourth straight title in 1939, but they would do it without the Iron Horse.

"That was a pretty good club [in 1938]. Henrich and DiMag were just starting out, but fit right in with the Yankees tradition. When I came up years later, you knew they took winning seriously. They took the tradition seriously."

—Yogi Berra

New York Mayor Fiorello LaGuardia offers hitting tips to Lefty Gomez (left) and Bill Dickey during the 1938 World Series at Chicago's Wrigley Field.

# Four Years of Dominance

Many baseball historians claim that the 1936-39 Yankees, winners of four straight world titles, are the greatest team ever assembled—and they have the numbers to back it up.

| | Record | Games Ahead | Runs (AL Rank) | Runs Allowed (AL Rank) | World Series |
|---|---|---|---|---|---|
| 1936 Yankees | 102-51 | 19.5 | 1,065 (1) | 731 (1) | 4-2 |
| 1937 Yankees | 102-52 | 13 | 979 (1) | 671 (1) | 4-1 |
| 1938 Yankees | 99-53 | 9.5 | 966 (1) | 710 (1) | 4-0 |
| 1939 Yankees | 106-45 | 17 | 967 (1) | 556 (1) | 4-0 |

# It's Yankees in a Thriller

## October 8, 1947

Pitcher Bill Bevens walks to the clubhouse after suffering one of the worst defeats in baseball history. Though he had a no-hitter with two outs in the ninth in Game 4, he lost the no-hit bid and the game, 3-2.

**Opposite Page:** Phil Rizzuto scores an important insurance run in the sixth inning of Game 7 of the World Series. After four heart-pounding games, the Yankees enjoyed a comfortable 5-2 victory in the finale.

Could it get any more dramatic than this? Some 71,548 souls jammed into Yankee Stadium on this sunny afternoon, not knowing what to expect—and how could they? They were there to witness Game 7 of an instant classic, this first postwar World Series between the Dodgers and Yankees. The first six games had remarkable heartbreak and implausible heroes. Fans had breathlessly followed every pitch throughout the baseball-crazed metropolis, most glued to the radio, others watching on the grainy images of a newfangled force known as television, as NBC brought the World Series into fans' living rooms for the first time. Less than five months earlier, the Dodgers had brought up a black man named Jack Roosevelt Robinson to play first base, ending baseball's segregation. The legendary broadcaster Red Barber would later title his book about Robinson and the historic '47 season *When All Hell Broke Loose.*

Certainly all-time attendance records were breaking at Yankee Stadium. In Game 6 of the '47 Series, a record 74,065 fans shoehorned their way into the House That Ruth Built, many paying $4 for the privilege of standing on the second-tier grillwork. What they saw were unforgettable moments, including journeyman outfielder Al Gionfriddo's acrobatic catch off a Joe DiMaggio drive toward the left-field bullpen gate, 415 feet away, to preserve an 8-6 victory, immortalized by Barber's trademark call, "Ohhhh doctor!"

Only three days earlier in Ebbets Field, another Brooklyn journeyman, Cookie Lavagetto, had broken up Yankees starter Bill Bevens' no-hit bid in the ninth. With two outs and two men on, Lavagetto laced a two-run double, giving Brooklyn a stunning 3-2, walk-off victory. It was a moment that triggered a raucous celebration and has been replayed as much as any one play in baseball history. (Ironically, the names Gionfriddo, Bevens, and Lavagetto never appeared in a major-league box score after the 1947 Series—all were toiling in the minors in '48 and were soon out of baseball.)

With such unexpected heroes and drama, the stage was set for Game 7. Both teams had exhausted pitching staffs. Yankees manager Bucky Harris, who won a world championship in Washington in 1924 but little else in his managerial career, opted to start rookie Spec

> "Nineteen forty-seven, that was my rookie year, my first Series, and it wasn't boring. I hit the first pinch-hit homer in the World Series. The next day I caught Bill Bevens, who was one out from a no-hitter. I felt bad he lost the no-hitter and the game. At least we won when it mattered."
>
> —Yogi Berra

Shea on one day's rest. Dodgers skipper Burt Shotton, a mild-mannered gent who managed in civilian clothes and a bow tie, went with Hal Gregg.

Brooklyn got to Shea early, but the Yankees went ahead in the fourth inning on two-out hits by Phil Rizzuto, Bobby Brown, and Tommy Henrich. Flame-throwing reliever Joe Page came in and sealed the deal with five sterling innings of one-hit ball, giving the Yankees a 5-2 victory and a hard-fought championship.

Compared to what had happened earlier, the Game 7 finale seemed almost anticlimactic. "After all the delirious, exciting, and unbelievable baseball that has been displayed," Arthur Daley wrote in *The New York Times*, "this was just a routing, businesslike job by a coldly efficient team."

Yet the 1947 World Series, played in the stadium haze and wafts of smoke created by record crowds, remains one for the ages. It was an achievement not taken lightly in the Yankees clubhouse, moments after Bruce Edwards grounded

The Yankees' $10,000 victory party at the Biltmore Hotel following Game 7 of the 1947 World Series was not exactly a mellow affair. It could've been called "Executive Gone Wild," and it changed the course of Yankees history.

The executive was Larry MacPhail, the Yankees' abrasive president, treasurer, and general manager. He had come to the Bronx in 1945 with a reputation as an energetic and temperamental innovator, and he quickly revitalized the franchise, including modernizing Yankee Stadium, at a cost of $600,000.

MacPhail, who had pioneered night baseball in the majors in 1935 in Cincinnati, installed lights in Yankee Stadium in 1946. He also offered women ushers at the stadium, popularized Old-Timers' Day, created a luxurious Stadium Club for season-ticket holders, moved the home dugout to the first-base side, and refurbished the clubhouse and press box.

MacPhail's hard-charging way of doing things wasn't the traditional Yankees approach. But he surely got results. He arranged the first major-league television contract, at a time when there were about 500 television sets in New York City. And under his stewardship, the Yankees drew 2.2 million in attendance in 1946, doubling the previous mark and making them the first team to break the two-million mark.

But MacPhail was also impulsive; he went through three managers in '46. And he was also a petty tyrant, prone to rages; he berated his own players during the '47 season. Right as the World Series ended, MacPhail, with beer bottle in hand, screamed, "That's it. That does it. That's my retirement!"

As James Dawson reported in *The New York Times*, "Larry MacPhail was shouting at the top of his lungs in an emotional outburst, tears streaming down his face as the curtain descended on the 1947 World Series."

At the hotel victory party, MacPhail made one last roaring appearance. He punched his former road secretary John McDonald and fired Yankees farm director George Weiss on the spot. He then got in a heated argument with co-owner Dan Topping. When the dust finally settled, Topping and Del Webb announced that they had purchased MacPhail's one-third share of the Yankees for $2 million. They also reinstated Weiss, the brilliant architect of future Yankees championships, as general manager.

Larry MacPhail, baseball's mad genius, had left the building.

**Opposite Page:** Joe DiMaggio crosses the plate with his fifth-inning home run during Game 3 of the World Series. The Dodgers had taken a 6-0 lead in the second inning and held on for a 9-8 victory.

Joe Page (center) runs off the field after securing New York's 5-3 victory in Game 1. Page also won the finale, 5-2, with five innings of one-hit, shutout ball.

into the Series-ending double play. Yankees players whooped and hollered, hugged and mugged for cameras, drank and sprayed champagne.

The Yankees had launched their new dynasty. They defeated the team that would become their most dramatic rival. The 1947 Series had ushered in the golden age of baseball, and Yankee Stadium—which held crowds of over two million in each of the next three years—would provide the stage for a whole lot more drama.

# Bombers Broom the Phils

## October 7, 1950

After winning a 1-0 squeaker in Game 1 of the 1950 fall classic, the Yankees took the second game 2-1 thanks to a 10th-inning home run by Joe DiMaggio, shown celebrating after the win.

**Opposite Page:** With the score 2-2 in the top of the ninth inning of Game 3, Yogi Berra tags out Granny Hamner. It was the second straight game in which the Phillies had blown a great chance for victory in the ninth inning.

Was the 1950 World Series someone's idea of a joke? Whiz Kids vs. Bronx Bombers? A team that hadn't won a pennant in 35 years against a team that practically invented the fall classic? Did the upstart Philadelphia Phillies really belong on the same field as the vaunted New York Yankees?

Speaking of fields, even the ballparks reflected the apparent mismatch—double-decked Shibe Park had less than half the capacity of triple-tiered Yankee Stadium. In fact, Yankee Stadium was the first triple-tiered park and among the first to be called a stadium.

All this mattered none to Philadelphians, who were delirious over their brash, young heroes. When the Whiz Kids dramatically fended off the Brooklyn Dodgers for their first pennant since the Woodrow Wilson administration, so began wild celebrations and a mad rush on Series tickets.

Amid all the giddy chaos, the Phillies somehow forgot to sell thousands of seats, so an entire grandstand of Shibe Park was left empty during the '50 Series. Who could imagine such a mishap ever happening at Yankee Stadium?

Under manager Eddie Sawyer, the Phillies entered October flushed with excitement, but also banged up and exhausted. Reliever Jim Konstanty was chosen to start Game 1 against 21-game winner Vic Raschi in Shibe Park. Raschi, of course, was part of the best and deepest pitching in baseball. And that's what ultimately won out in a four-game sweep that wasn't quite the joke people had expected.

The Yankees had four hitters over .300, including league MVP Phil Rizzuto at .324, Yogi Berra .322, Hank Bauer .320, and Joe DiMaggio .301, but the Phillies pretty much kept the Bronx batsmen in check. The difference was the Yankees' arms, which overpowered the Phillies' hitters, combining for a Series ERA of 0.73 and allowing only five runs in the four games. They turned the Whiz Kids into the Fizz Kids.

Yet the lowest-scoring World Series wasn't without its moments. Game 2 featured a classic pitching duel between Allie Reynolds and the Phillies' Robin Roberts, tied 1-1 after nine innings. It was decided in the 10th inning by DiMaggio's homer off Roberts, who would

"Reporters thought I'd be nervous, a rookie pitching in the World Series. I told them I don't get butterflies. I was more worried about finding 60 or 70 tickets for my friends and family."

—Whitey Ford

win 286 games over his Hall of Fame career, but never appeared in another World Series.

In Game 3 at the Stadium, the Phillies gave the Yankees all they could handle, until shortstop Granny Hamner's costly error in the eighth enabled the Yankees to tie the game. Hamner was so inconsolable that DiMaggio tried to encourage him the next day, reminding him he was too good a player to blame himself.

But the Yankees were simply too good, period. "The Yankees needed pitching and got it," wrote Milton Gross in the *New York Post*. "They needed the big hit and DiMag produced it. When they needed the big defensive play, someone was there to make it."

In Game 4 before a lively stadium crowd of 68,098, the Yankees gave the ball to Ed "Whitey" Ford, the 21-year-old rookie from Astoria in Queens, New York, who had a large rooting section of family and friends. Ford did not disappoint, taking a 5-0 lead into the ninth.

Yet with two outs and two on, left fielder Gene Woodling lost a fly in the stadium shadows, and two runs scored. Taking no chances, Casey Stengel brought in Reynolds to replace Ford, a move greeted by thunderous boos. "Hell, half of them were my relatives anyway," Ford later recalled. "But I'll never forget Reynolds coming in; he was the meanest-looking pitcher I ever saw, and it was October and it was getting tough to see the ball in the stadium with that haze, and besides it was late afternoon and getting dark."

Reynolds fired three fastballs past big Stan Lopata, and it was lights out for the Phillies. But there was no shame in losing to the Yankees. According to Jimmy Powers, the Whiz Kids took "a quietly efficient, very dignified, and very thorough beating."

Gene Woodling scores the winning run in the bottom of the ninth inning of Game 3. With two outs, Woodling singled, went to second on a Phil Rizzuto single, and came home on a hit by Jerry Coleman.

Whitey Ford pitched a gem in the Game 4 clincher, a 5-2 Yankees victory. The young southpaw tallied eight shutout innings before allowing two unearned runs in the ninth.

"That was my second year, and probably my best. We swept Philadelphia in the Series, but it wasn't as easy as it looked. Every game was tight except for the last. What I remember most is every time I came up, we had a chance to score and I was lucky enough to deliver."

—Jerry Coleman

In his first full season in the American League, 37-year-old slugger Johnny Mize (right) powered the 1950 Yankees with 25 home runs and 72 RBI in just 90 games and only 274 at-bats.

# Scooter's Fab '50

For more than half a century, Phil Rizzuto was a colorful and popular fixture at Yankee Stadium, first as a sparkplug shortstop on eight world championship teams, then in the broadcast booth as an unabashed homer.

Many remember him for silly superstitions, cannolism, and "Holy Cows." Others remember him as the first mystery guest on the classic game show *What's My Line?* or for his play-by-play on Meat Loaf's hit single, "Paradise by the Dashboard Light."

To his teammates, he's simply remembered as being indispensable.

As Tommy Henrich noted during the 1950 season, "This ballclub can get along without me or anyone else—except one. We just keep praying that nothing happens to that little scamp at shortstop. He's the one we have to have every day."

It was little wonder why the long-underrated 5-foot-6, 150-pound Rizzuto was named the American League's Most Valuable Player that season. He played the best ball of his outstanding career, which began before World War II.

The Scooter could turn the double play like no other. From September 1949 to June 1950, he played 58 consecutive games without an error, handling 288 chances flawlessly. He also bunted often and effectively, led the league in sacrifices that year, and still hit a career-best .324.

Not bad for a pint-sized kid from Brooklyn, who was once rejected by the Dodgers and Giants after tryouts. In fact, then-Dodgers manager Casey Stengel told him, "You're too small. Go get a shoebox."

Yet Rizzuto, who attended his first game at Yankee Stadium as a 10-year-old, sitting in the right-field bleachers, never lost faith. And he ultimately gained the admiration of Stengel, for whom Scooter played his best seasons. "He is the greatest shortstop I have ever seen in my entire baseball career, and I have watched some beauties," the Yankees manager once said. "If I were a retired gentleman, I would follow the Yankees around just to see Rizzuto work those miracles every day."

Miracle or not, Rizzuto is enshrined in the Baseball Hall of Fame, his No. 10 retired by the Yankees, and has a plaque in Monument Park. It fittingly reads, "A Man's Size Is Measured by His Heart."

69

# Bauer Triples the Fun

## October 10, 1951

Hank Bauer cracks a three-bagger in the sixth inning of Game 6. The hit plated Hall of Famers Yogi Berra, Joe DiMaggio, and Johnny Mize and gave New York a 4-1 lead.

**Opposite Page:** Italian-American teammates Phil Rizzuto (left) and Yogi Berra smooch Hank Bauer after his heroics in the Game 6 clincher. As a Marine six years earlier, Bauer was fighting the Japanese on Okinawa.

Seated among the Polo Grounds crowd for the epic Dodgers-Giants playoff game on October 3, 1951, were several members of the New York Yankees, there strictly as impartial observers.

Well, not exactly. The Yankees, who had already clinched their third consecutive pennant, were there to discover their eventual opponent in the World Series. Later, many admitted they were rooting for the Giants since the Polo Grounds (55,000 seats) had a larger capacity than Ebbets Field (32,000), meaning there would be a larger World Series share for the winners.

So Bobby Thomson's "Shot Heard 'Round the World" didn't terribly disappoint the Yankees, who had previously called the Polo Grounds home, from 1913-22, before moving across the Harlem River to their own ballpark, when Yankee Stadium opened in 1923.

For a dime fare, the '51 Subway Series had storylines galore. It was the first confrontation between the ballyhooed rookie outfielders, Willie Mays and Mickey Mantle. The Giants played the first all-black outfield in history—Mays, Monte Irvin, and Hank Thompson. And the Series would mark the final appearances of 36-year-old Joe DiMaggio.

The high-flying Giants, still riding the euphoria from Thomson's heroics, captured Game 1, thanks to Irvin's four hits and steal of home. Although the Yankees won Game 2, it was a costly victory. Mantle, playing right field, caught his spikes on a drain cover in right-center at the stadium, injuring his knee and taking him out of the Series. The injury would hamper him for the rest of his career.

After the Giants won Game 3—highlighted by Eddie Stanky's controversial kicking of the ball out of Phil Rizzuto's glove on a play at second—the Yankees' vaunted pitching went to work. Allie Reynolds and Eddie Lopat won the next two. And in Game 6 at the stadium, Hank Bauer, a hard-nosed clutch player once voted by his teammates the "man most likely to succeed in a free-for-all," lived up to his nickname, "Man of the Hour."

Playing right in place of Mantle, Bauer benefited from a tricky Yankee Stadium wind— as well as the umpire's generous call of a ball on Dave Koslo's two-strike pitch— to belt

"Right after we win the Series, I get this call saying the Marines need experienced pilots to serve in Korea. I was an inactive reservist and hadn't really thought about it—I'm playing baseball, right? But the guy tells me, 'We're going to get you for a year and a half.' So I told him, 'Do me a favor. Take me right now.' And I served through 1953 and flew 66 missions."

—Jerry Coleman

a bases-loaded triple in the sixth inning that would be the difference. "When the wind blew in and hit that top bleacher, it blew back out again. Like a jet stream," he later recalled.

"Monte Irvin in left field didn't know that. He had been playing me shallow, and when the ball took off, he couldn't get back in time. It hit the 402 mark for a three-run triple. I did have to hit the ball, but it goes to show you how much difference a little luck can make. If the umpire calls that pitch correctly, I'm out. We don't score those runs. Instead we make the lead hold up and win the Series."

Bauer also ensured that the lead held up. Trailing 4-1 in the ninth, the Giants loaded the bases with no outs. Enter reliever Bob Kuzava, acquired in June from the Washington Senators. After two sacrifice flies and the score now 4-3, pinch hitter Sal Yvars hit a sinking liner to right. The stadium crowd gasped as Bauer momentarily lost the ball in the crowd's white shirts and the shadows. But he relocated it and charged forward. Bauer, who played in nine World Series and always came through when it mattered most, slid on his knees to catch the ball inches off the ground. Game over, 1951 World Series over. The Yankees win again.

Three Bombers score on Bauer's famous triple in the sixth inning of Game 6. More than 61,000 fans were on hand to witness the historic clout.

Allie Reynolds (left) and Joe DiMaggio celebrate a 6-2 win in Game 4. Reynolds won for the first time since his September 28 no-hitter, and DiMaggio belted his last career home run.

"What do I remember about that year? It should've been my second season in the majors, but I was in the army and got married that April. The Yankees asked me to delay my honeymoon plans so I could throw out the first pitch on Opening Day, wearing my army uniform. I was flattered, and Joan said okay, so that was my only pitch of the '51 season."

—Whitey Ford

# The Mick's Debut

From the moment he first stepped into the triple-tiered palace in the Bronx on the chilly afternoon of April 17, 1951, Mickey Charles Mantle knew he was light years from Spavinaw, Oklahoma.

He was only 19 years old, hadn't slept the night before, and was trembling with fear. "It was the worst day of my life," he would recall.

Only weeks earlier, Mantle was in Yankees spring training, supposedly for a look-see, destined for seasoning in the minor leagues. But the shortstop-turned-outfielder's sensational 500-foot homers that spring changed Casey Stengel's thinking. He was the talk of the town and all of baseball, and was now in Yankee Stadium for Opening Day 1951.

Many of the stadium crowd of 44,860 came early, just to watch this much-hyped slugger in batting practice. He was wearing No. 6, apparently designed to follow the lineage of Yankees greats Ruth (3), Gehrig (4), and DiMaggio (5). (He would change his number to 7 later in the year.)

Before the game, reporters asked Yankees coach Bill Dickey, a former teammate of the aforementioned trio of greats, for his opinion on the shy phenom. "He's green," Dickey said. "But he's got to be great. All that power, a switch-hitter, and he runs like a striped ape. If he drags a bunt past the pitcher, he's on base. I think he's the fastest man I ever saw with the Yankees."

When the game began, Mantle ultimately calmed down. He batted third and played right field in his major-league debut, going 1-for-4, including an RBI single as the Yankees blanked the Red Sox 5-0 behind Vic Raschi's pitching.

Ironically, another future legend was also making his Yankee Stadium debut on the same day. It was Bob Sheppard, the new public address announcer, whose distinguished and unmistakable voice would define the stadium for generations. Before he died in 1995, Mantle said hearing Sheppard pronounce his name used to give him goosebumps. And Sheppard admitted he also got goosebumps when he said the words "Mickey Mantle."

# High Five

## October 5, 1953

Going into Game 6 of the World Series, Yankees manager Casey Stengel was upbeat about his team's chances of winning their 16th World Series title. And why wouldn't he be? After all, the Yankees had just trounced their crosstown rivals, the Brooklyn Dodgers, in Game 5, with an 11-7 victory.

Granted, the Dodgers had outhit the Yankees 14-11 at Ebbets Field, but the Yankees had accumulated four home runs to only two by the Dodgers. One of the bombs had been Mickey Mantle's opposite-field grand slam, which effectively took some of the wind from the Dodgers' sail. Stengel liked his team's chances because they held a 3-2 Series edge and because they were going back to the Bronx to play the final two games—if two were even necessary—at Yankee Stadium.

Stengel was also genuinely fond of the team, which included Mantle, Yogi Berra, Phil Rizzuto, Hank Bauer, and Gil McDougald pacing the starting lineup, and Whitey Ford, Johnny Sain, Vic Raschi, Allie Reynolds, and Eddie Lopat boosting the pitching staff. And to top it off, Stengel's favorite Yankee, second baseman Billy Martin, was playing better than ever.

Martin, who had batted just .257 during the 1953 regular season, was dismantling Dodgers pitching. In the previous year's World Series, Martin had used his glove to make a rally-killing play in Game 7 to help put the Dodgers away. A year later, his red-hot bat produced a three-run triple and two other hits to lead a 9-5 Yankees win in Game 1. The fiery Martin hit a solo home run in Game 2 that had tied the score in the seventh in a 4-2 Yankees victory.

When the Series moved to Brooklyn, the Dodgers took Games 3 and 4 before Martin added to the Yankees' assault in Game 5 with a home run.

Stengel had other reasons to want the Yankees to win Game 6 and thereby claim the World Series. If the Yankees managed to do so, they would become the first team in major-league history to win five consecutive World Series.

However, Brooklyn could not be so easily dismissed. Managed by Chuck Dressen, the

The Series was tied at two games apiece when the Yankees won Game 5 at Ebbets Field, 11-7. Mantle (pictured) was one of four Bombers to go yard in the game.

**Opposite Page:** Coach Frank Crosetti (No. 2) hugs Billy Martin after the Yankees won Game 6 by the score of 4-3 to win the Series. Martin cracked 12 hits in the fall classic to capture MVP honors.

"When fans would come to games at Fenway Park or Ebbets Field, they'd bring gloves. When they came to the stadium, they'd bring binoculars. Naturally I enjoyed pitching in Yankee Stadium."

—Whitey Ford

Dodgers had a lineup that included Carl Furillo, Roy Campanella, Gil Hodges, Duke Snider, and Jackie Robinson. Carl Erskine led a quality pitching staff that included Preacher Roe, Billy Loes, and Russ Meyer.

Hoping to avoid the team's seventh World Series loss in seven appearances, the Dodgers sent Erskine to the mound on two days' rest to start Game 6. Erskine had pitched Game 3 in Brooklyn and handcuffed the Yankees, allowing two runs on six hits while striking out 14 to take a complete-game victory. Whitey Ford started for the Yankees, and if a big game needed to be won, the Yankees left-hander seemed to have an edge.

A crowd of 62,370 filled Yankee Stadium and watched with delight when the Yankees scored two runs in the first, thanks in part to a crucial

This image diagrams Billy Martin's triple in the first inning of Game 1 at Yankee Stadium. The three-run blow scored Hank Bauer, Mickey Mantle, and Gene Woodling and keyed a 9-5 New York victory.

Brooklyn's Jim Gilliam crashes into Billy Martin but is out at second base. Defense was a key factor in this Series. Brooklyn committed seven errors; New York one.

error by Junior Gilliam on a ball hit by—who else?—Martin.

Erskine hurt himself in the second inning, when his throwing error helped the Yankees increase the lead to 3-0. He added two scoreless innings before leaving the game after four innings. Meanwhile, Ford held the Dodgers scoreless for five innings before they pushed across their first run in the sixth, when Robinson doubled, stole third, and scored on a groundout.

Holding a 3-1 lead, Reynolds was brought in to relieve Ford and he retired the Dodgers in the eighth, before finding trouble in the ninth. After walking Snider, Furillo hit a two-run homer into the right-field stands to tie the game at three.

Had the Yankees' run hit a streak of bad luck? Surely no team could win five straight World Series—the baseball gods could not be so kind to any one team.

Hoping to hold the Yankees and force the game into extra innings, Clem Labine went to

> "I played for a guy, Casey Stengel, who was on my butt all the time because, I figured, he knew I could be a pretty good player. And you know, I've got six World Series rings because of that."
>
> —Moose Skowron

the mound to start his third inning of relief. Unfortunately for the Dodgers, Bauer walked to lead off the inning. After Berra lined out to right field, Mantle beat out an infield hit to put runners at first and second.

Over the years, Yankee Stadium had seen the likes of sluggers such as Babe Ruth, Lou Gehrig, and Joe DiMaggio, but no Yankee from the past could have looked more imposing to the Dodgers than the next man up to bat.

Martin stepped to the plate with a chance to win the World Series with one swing of his bat. And he delivered a single up the middle to bring Bauer home with the winning run.

Martin's 12th hit of the World Series produced his eighth RBI and the Yankees' unprecedented fifth consecutive World Series win.

# Six in a Row?

The Yankees had just won their fifth consecutive World Series and Yankees manager Casey Stengel had already moved on to the 1954 season. Thinking out loud, Stengel talked about the prospect of winning a sixth consecutive World Series. After all, he still had the nucleus of a team that had just finished winning a record five straight.

What he didn't see on the horizon were the Cleveland Indians.

Managed by Al Lopez, the Indians had a stellar pitching staff led by Early Wynn and Bob Lemon. The Indians got ahead by a large margin, but after taking two out of three from the Indians at Yankee Stadium from August 31 to September 2, the Yankees felt they could once again take the crown.

A critical doubleheader on September 12 at Cleveland's Municipal Stadium loomed large. At the time, the Indians held a 6½ game lead on the Yankees. If the Yankees could somehow sweep, they knew they would cut the lead to 4½ and put immense pressure on Lopez's troops.

A record crowd of 86,563 showed up to support the Indians, who sent Wynn and Lemon to the mound. And the Yankees lost 4-1 and 3-2, allowing the Indians to push their American League lead to 8½ games, with just 10 games remaining on the Indians' schedule. The champs had been dethroned and they knew it.

The Yankees finished eight games behind the Indians, who posted a record of 111-43. Meanwhile, the Yankees won 100 games for the first time under Stengel.

# Larsen's Masterpiece

## October 8, 1956

Late in the 1956 campaign, Larsen was forced to adopt a no-windup delivery to stop batters from detecting whether he was throwing a fastball or a curve.

**Opposite Page:** Usually, the catcher jumps into the pitcher's arms, but Yogi Berra couldn't contain himself. After all, he had just become the first player ever to catch a perfect game in the World Series!

Don Larsen pitched one of the worst games in the history of the World Series … in Game 2, that is. Facing Brooklyn in the 1956 fall classic, Larsen was so wild—allowing four walks and four runs—that manager Casey Stengel pulled him in the second inning. "I was lousy in my first start," Larsen recalled. "I was ahead 6-0 when I started walking people. Casey didn't like that…. I didn't think I'd start another game."

With the Series deadlocked at two games apiece, Stengel was unsure who would start the pivotal Game 5 at Yankee Stadium. Many Yankees fans hoped it wouldn't be Larsen. For Baltimore in 1954, he had gone 3-21. And even though he had posted an 11-5 record for New York in 1956, he had allowed a whopping average of 4.8 walks per game. After the Game 2 fiasco, Larsen didn't expect to start again. The night before Game 5, he drank a couple of beers before bed.

When he arrived at the stadium on Monday, Larsen saw that a baseball had been placed on his spikes—the sign that Stengel had chosen him to start. Larsen wondered if his eccentric manager had made the right decision. "After what I did in Brooklyn, he could have forgotten about me, and who would blame him?" he said.

Nonetheless, Larsen appeared nonchalant and composed as he took the hill against the Dodgers lineup, which featured such stars as Jackie Robinson, Roy Campanella, and Duke Snider. Relying on catcher Yogi Berra's calls, the hulking, slouch-shouldered right-hander went to work. In the top of the first, he struck out the first two batters, Junior Gilliam and Pee Wee Reese, on called third strikes. In the early innings, he threw with uncharacteristic precision. By the fourth, he had retired all 12 men he had faced.

Mickey Mantle put the Yankees up 1-0 with a home run in the fourth inning, then made a terrific backhanded catch of a Gil Hodges' smash in the fifth. Following two Brooklyn popouts and a strikeout in the sixth, Larsen maintained his perfect game.

After the Yankees went ahead 2-0 in the sixth, the buzz among the monstrous crowd of 64,519 spectators began to build—and the Dodgers began to worry. The 6-foot-4 Larsen loomed large, as did the afternoon shadows, which made it more difficult to see

"Mantle made a beautiful catch. That ball probably would have been a home run in most parks, but Yankee Stadium at that time was pretty big in left-center. Mantle could run like a deer. When he caught that ball I had a sigh of relief."

—Don Larsen

the ball. Leading off the seventh, Gilliam nearly banged out a hit, but shortstop Gil McDougald made a good play for out number one. Larsen then retired Reese and Snider on outfield flies.

In the bottom of the seventh, Larsen ventured to the runway area of the Yankees dugout for a quick smoke. Spotting Mantle, he said, "Do you think I'll make it, Mick?" Mantle was startled. According to tradition, when a pitcher has a no-hitter going, no one is supposed talk to him—especially when it's a perfect game in the World Series. "I tried to engage in conversation with some of our players on the bench during the game, but they all avoided me like the plague …," Larsen said in a 2003 interview with *Baseball Digest*. "I was the loneliest guy on the bench. Nobody would talk to me."

In the top of the eighth, the tension mounted. Recalled Joseph Reichler of the Associated Press, "By the eighth inning, every pitch brought an explosive gasp from the crowd, followed by a nervous, incomprehensible babbling that seemed to sweep through the stands in waves."

Robinson opened the eighth by bouncing out to Larsen. Hodges then sent an electric shock through the crowd with a low liner to the hole, but third sacker Andy Carey snatched it just inches off the ground. Sandy Amoros then flied out to center to end the inning.

In the bottom of the eighth, close to 100 million Americans were tuned into the game on radio. Fans rose to their feet when Larsen came to the plate, and didn't jeer when he struck out against Sal Maglie. Entering the final inning, the Yankees maintained a 2-0 lead.

In the top of the ninth, Larsen was jittery with anxiety. Nevertheless, he got Carl Furillo to fly out to right. The next hitter, Campanella, "hit a drive that I was sure would be a home run," Larsen said. "But it curved foul at the last second. I was so nervous, I almost fell down. My legs were rubbery, and my fingers didn't feel like they were on my hand. I said to myself, 'Please help me out, somebody.'"

As it turned out, Larsen didn't need much help. Campanella hit an easy grounder to second baseman Billy Martin, who gunned him down. Larsen was now just one out away from the first no-hitter, let alone a perfect game, in World Series history. Pinch hitter Dale Mitchell, a career .312 hitter, stepped to the plate. "My legs were shaking," Larsen said. "I thought, 'Just get me through one more.'

To get that close and mess it up, they'd run me out of the ballpark."

Larsen's first pitch was a ball outside, but he came back with a slider for a strike and then a swing and a miss. He was now just one strike away from immortality. Mitchell swung at the next pitch … but fouled it into the stands. With the count 1-2, Berra called for a fastball. Larsen hadn't waved off his catcher all day, and he wasn't about to now. He reared back and fired a blazer on the outside corner. As Mitchell stood frozen, umpire Babe Pinelli thumbed him out.

Yankee Stadium erupted in perhaps its loudest cheer ever. Berra ran to the mound and jumped into his pitcher's arms. Larsen's teammates hugged him, slapped him, and shook his hand, as some fans jumped onto the field to congratulate him. "It can't be true," Larsen told United Press after the game. "Any minute now I expect the alarm clock to ring and someone to say, 'Okay Larsen, it's time to get up.'"

But he wasn't dreaming. Don Larsen had achieved the ultimate pitching feat: a perfect game in the World Series. To this day, it is considered the greatest moment in the history of the Yankees, if not all of Major League Baseball.

"I was 16 years old, and a junior at St. Francis Prep in Brooklyn. My brother, Frank, was playing for the Milwaukee Braves and he secured two tickets for me to Game 5. We sat in the upper deck in left field about midway between third base and the foul pole. When Mickey Mantle made that running catch in the fifth inning, it looked as though he was running toward us."

—Joe Torre

**Opposite Page:** The most significant numbers on this scoreboard were the zero under the H for Brooklyn and the goose egg under the E for the Yankees. Uncharacteristically, Larsen didn't walk anybody, either.

Casey Stengel praises Larsen in the locker room after the perfect game. Stengel deserved credit for starting Larsen in Game 5 after he had allowed four walks and four runs in less than two innings in Game 2.

## The 27 Outs A batter-by-batter rundown of Larsen's perfect game

**First Inning:**
Junior Gilliam strikes out.
Pee Wee Reese strikes out.
Duke Snider lines out to RF.

**Second Inning:**
Jackie Robinson grounds out to SS.
Gil Hodges strikes out.
Sandy Amoros pops out to 2B.

**Third Inning:**
Carl Furillo flies out to RF.
Roy Campanella strikes out.
Sal Maglie lines out to CF.

**Fourth Inning:**
Gilliam grounds out to 2B.
Reese grounds out to 2B.
Snider strikes out.

**Fifth Inning:**
Robinson flies out to RF.
Hodges flies out to CF.
Amoros grounds out to 2B.

**Sixth Inning:**
Furillo pops out to 2B.
Campanella pops out to 2B.
Maglie strikes out.

**Seventh Inning:**
Gilliam grounds out to SS.
Reese flies out to CF.
Snider flies out to LF.

**Eighth Inning:**
Robinson grounds out to P.
Hodges lines out to 3B.
Amoros flies out to CF.

**Ninth Inning:**
Furillo flies out to RF.
Campanella grounds out to 2B.
Dale Mitchell strikes out.

81

# Chambliss' Pennant-Winning Pop

## October 14, 1976

Chambliss had quietly amassed 96 RBI in his breakout season in 1976, but only with this series-clinching clout did he become a household name.

**Opposite Page:** With his epic home run, Chris Chambliss joined Bobby Thomson and Bill Mazeroski as players who climaxed a postseason series with a walk-off home run.

Yankee Stadium without the postseason felt strange, but the drought had reached 12 years in 1976.

Not since the 1964 World Series, when the Yankees lost to the Cardinals in seven games, had the most storied franchise in sports been to the postseason. There were no championship series or designated hitters the last time Yankee Stadium hosted a World Series. Regular-season games determined what teams from the American and National Leagues would play one another in the World Series, and pitchers hit for themselves.

So Yankee Stadium—which had been shut down the previous two years for a major face-lift—felt like a modern-day Brigadoon that had sprung back to life after a 100-year slumber. And true to form, Yankee Stadium served as the site for the deciding fifth game of the American League Championship Series, between the Yankees of the American League East division and the Kansas City Royals of the American League West.

A classic contrast between the two teams could be seen all the way down to their uniforms. The Yankees wore their traditional pinstripes, while the Royals donned powder blue double knits. The Yankees were the most successful franchise in the history of Major League Baseball; the Royals were an expansion team that came into being in 1969. The Royals were built from within and they had talented players, such as third baseman George Brett, who was generally regarded as the American League's best young player. Each club had a quality skipper, with Billy Martin managing the Yankees and Whitey Herzog the Royals.

Catfish Hunter successfully pitched the Yankees to a 4-1 win in the opening game of the series. However, KC won Games 2 and 4 to tie it up.

Martin opted to start Ed Figueroa on three days' rest in Game 5 on October 14, a decision easily second-guessed, since Doyle Alexander and Ken Holtzman were well rested and available to start. Part of the decision to start Figueroa had been his performance in Game 2, while the other part of the decision came down to Martin's disapproval of Steinbrenner's trading for Alexander and Holtzman.

"Hitting the home run off [Mark] Littell to win the pennant was the most satisfying moment of my career because I know what it meant to my teammates—our first pennant since 1964. As soon as the ball sailed over the right-field fence, it was a crazy, wild scene, fans mobbing everywhere. I didn't touch home plate because it wasn't there to touch."

—Chris Chambliss

Third baseman Graig Nettles belted two home runs at home in Game 4 of the ALCS, but the Royals won 7-4 to even the best-of-five series at two games apiece.

Fans poured onto the field so fast after Chambliss' homer that he had to fight through the crowd to reach home plate—and then the dugout. "Scary," is how he put it.

The Royals jumped on Figueroa to score twice in the first inning on John Mayberry's home run. But Figueroa survived, and the Yankees came back to build a 6-3 lead after seven innings. A partisan Yankee Stadium crowd smelled a coming date in the World Series against the Cincinnati Reds. But the Royals weren't done just yet.

A leadoff single to start the eighth chased Figueroa in favor of left-hander Grant Jackson. Herzog went to pinch hitter Jim Wohlford, who responded with a single to bring Brett to the plate.

Not only did Brett have talent; he also held a grudge against the Yankees. Brett's older brother Ken had been on the Yankees earlier in the season, and George did not like the way Ken had been treated by the Yankees, who later traded him to the Chicago White Sox.

Martin stuck with Jackson to pitch to the left-handed-hitting Brett. The decision proved fatal when Brett rerouted one of Jackson's pitches into the right-field stands to tie the game at 6-6 and effectively silence Yankee Stadium.

The Yankees survived the ninth, when the Royals got two aboard to bring Wohlford to the plate. Every Yankees fan understood the significance of this at-bat. If Wohlford succeeded, the Royals would likely take the lead. Even worse, if Wohlford got on base, Brett would get another opportunity to rock the Yankees' world.

Fortunately for the Yankees, they were able to end the inning on a fielder's choice.

Chris Chambliss led off the Yankees' ninth, stepping to the plate during the Yankees public address announcer's warning to unruly fans, who had peppered the field with debris.

"In 1973, my first year playing in old Yankee Stadium turned me into a pull hitter. I'd been a spray hitter at Cleveland. Since it was only 296 [feet] down the right-field line, that led me to adjust and I led the league in homers [in 1976]. I will say winning the pennant like we did that night was the most unbelievable thrill."

—Graig Nettles

With his team's fortunes hanging in the balance, Mark Littell stood on the mound for the Royals. The right-hander delivered, Chambliss swung, and Yankee Stadium erupted. Chambliss paused briefly after connecting. The ball landed in the right-field stands, and he began his trying journey around the bases.

Fans spilled onto the field. Some simply wanted to celebrate while others wanted to thank Chambliss for coming through. Chambliss fought to reach home, eventually receiving assistance from several New York police officers. When he reached home plate, the Yankees were officially headed to the World Series.

# The Lost Years: 1965-75

Prior to heading to the World Series in 1976, the Yankees had seen a lull in championships dating back to 1964, when the Yankees went to the World Series but lost in seven games to the St. Louis Cardinals.

While Yankee Stadium witnessed a lot of losing during the 11-year period between American League championships, the Yankees actually posted a winning record of 888-881 over that period. However, they had one 10th place finish, one ninth, a sixth, two fifths, three fourths, a third, and two seconds. The team's second-place finish in 1970 saw them post their best record of the period when they went 93-69, but finished 15 games behind the Orioles in the AL East division.

During the silent years at Yankee Stadium, the Yankees employed four managers: Johnny Keane, Ralph Houk, Bill Virdon, and Billy Martin. This period also saw great change in baseball, with the advent of the designated hitter, free agency, and divisional play. In addition, the Yankees spent the 1974 and 1975 seasons at Shea Stadium while Yankee Stadium was being remodeled.

Perhaps the most significant date during this time of great suffering for Yankees fans was January 3, 1973. That was the day George M. Steinbrenner, who headed a limited partnership, purchased the Yankees from CBS. The fiery owner of the Yankees, though often controversial, did what was necessary to bring winning back to the Bronx.

# Mr. October

### October 18, 1977

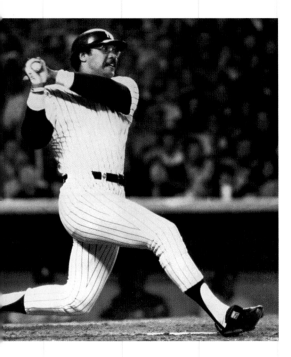

Excluding a first-inning walk in Game 6, Jackson homered in four straight at-bats— one in his last at-bat in Game 5 and three in Game 6.

**Opposite Page:** Reggie watches Charlie Hough's eighth-inning delivery sail deep into the night, more than 400 feet away. Not only had Reggie tied Babe Ruth's feat of three home runs in one World Series game, but he did it on three straight pitches.

Reggie Jackson had never been so humiliated. At Fenway Park on June 18, 1977, Yankees manager Billy Martin pulled his right fielder in the middle of an inning for supposedly loafing on a ball hit to the outfield. On a nationally televised Saturday afternoon game, Martin ordered Jackson to retreat to the dugout while Paul Blair took his place. Jackson and Martin exchanged hostile words before going after each other. Players and coaches prevented a potentially ugly fistfight.

According to some players, Martin overreacted, stating that the manager had had it in for the audacious slugger since the day the Yankees had acquired him as a free agent in November 1976. As Yankees catcher Fran Healy recalled, "[A]fter the Yankees signed Reggie, I was with Billy in the Yankee Stadium clubhouse. I remember him saying, 'I'll show him who's boss.'"

In a *Sport* magazine article before the 1977 season, Jackson asserted that he would be the man who would lead the Yankees to greatness. This statement ticked off catcher Thurman Munson, who not only captained the team but—as AL MVP—had led the Yankees to the 1976 World Series, in which he had batted .529 in a loss to Cincinnati. The hostility among Martin, Munson, Jackson, and others simmered all season, especially after the Fenway incident. Veteran baseball writer Roger Angell described the Yankees' clubhouse as the most joyless he had ever encountered.

New York wound up winning the AL East by 2½ games over Boston and Baltimore, Jackson's previous team. Some say that the Bombers prevailed not in spite of the Martin-Jackson feud, but partly because of it. A look at their track records confirms this assertion. Jackson's bravado had helped Oakland win three straight World Series (1972-74), while Martin's agitation had sparked the Twins, Tigers, and Yankees to division championships. Their volatile mix kept the team's juices flowing in 1977 and may well have contributed to their successful, 100-win campaign.

Nevertheless, Jackson did not enjoy his first season in the Bronx Zoo. Despite posting formidable numbers (.286-32-110), "I had been on a ball and chain all year, at least in my

mind," he wrote in his autobiography, *Reggie*. "I had heard so many negatives about Reggie Jackson. I had been the villain."

The summer of 1977 was troubling for the city in general. Serial killer David Berkowitz, "Son of Sam," was still on the loose after randomly killing six young people, wounding others, and terrifying millions. "I love to hunt," Berkowitz wrote. "Prowling the streets looking for fair game—tasty meat."

Hearing that the deranged killer preferred brunettes, dark-haired women donned blonde wigs. Greater panic arrived on the night of July 13-14, when the power went out throughout New York City. Amid the chaos, rioters and looters ransacked stores. Arsonists torched buildings, contributing to more than a thousand fires.

Having only played for small-market teams, Jackson found New York to be one crazy place. In the postseason, he faced mounting pressure from the merciless media. Through the ALCS (against Kansas

"It's still the greatest single-game performance I've ever seen. Really amazing. It was the sixth and final game and gave me chills when he hit that third one, which was hit even farther than the first two.... It didn't matter in the slightest whether you liked the Yanks or detested them. You put away whatever you felt for the team and just bathed in the magnitude of Reggie's achievement."

—Graig Nettles

City) and Game 2 of the World Series (versus the Dodgers), he was batting just .136. It was at this point that Munson facetiously dubbed him Mr. October. But from that point on, Jackson turned the sarcastic jab into a fitting moniker. He scored twice in a 5-3 victory in Game 3, then doubled and homered in a 4-2 triumph in Game 4. Although the Dodgers cruised 10-4 in Game 5, Jackson homered in his last at-bat.

When the Yankees returned home for Game 6, up three games to two, Jackson was ready to tee off. In batting practice, he whacked ball after ball out of the park. "Save some of those for the game," said Yankees second baseman Willie Randolph. "No problem," Jackson replied, full of confidence. "There are more where those came from."

The game began on a blustery Tuesday night, in the glow of a nearby fire. A few blocks from the ballpark, a five-alarm blaze enveloped an abandoned elementary school. ABC News cameras cut to the enflamed building, adding to the yearlong impression that the whole city was going to hell. Inside Yankee Stadium, 56,000 fans huddled as one.

Jackson looked for a pitch he could drive his first time up, but instead walked on four pitches. The Dodgers were looking to bust Jackson inside, but he adjusted, backing an inch or two away from the plate. In the fourth inning on Burt Hooton's first delivery, Jackson belted a two-run homer to give New York a 4-3 lead. In the fifth, he knocked Elias Sosa's first offering into the right-field seats. Counting his Game 5 homer, he had socked three home runs on three consecutive swings.

With New York up 7-3 in the eighth, and victory nearly assured, fans could hardly contain their excitement. Their 15-year thirst for a championship was about to be quenched. When Jackson stepped to the plate in the bottom of the eighth, fans rose to their feet, ecstatic. Their hard chant of "Reg-gie! Reg-gie! Reg-gie!" shook the house. And then, with a mighty rip at a Charlie Hough knuckleball (again, the first pitch!), Jackson blasted a moon shot into the night sky, making it 8-3, the final score. He flipped his bat and watched as the ball rocketed deep, deep to right-center, into the unoccupied bleachers, 475 feet away. "Oh, what a blow! ...," intoned ABC's Howard Cosell. "Oh, what a beam on his face. How can you blame him? He's answered the whole world!"

The new Mr. October had just joined Babe Ruth as the only sluggers to belt three home runs in a World Series game, and he had become the first man ever to club five round-trippers in a single fall classic.

"Reg-gie! Reg-gie! Reg-gie!" fans thundered, demanding a curtain call. Jackson bounded out of the dugout and waved his cap to his fans. "[S]uddenly I didn't care what the manager or my teammates had said or what the media had written...," Jackson wrote. "It was the happiest moment of my career."

Their midseason feud long behind them, Reggie and manager Billy Martin are all smiles during a post-championship news conference following Game 6.

Jackson makes a mad dash toward the dugout after helping the Yankees clinch their first world title in 15 years. Like the ALCS finale a year earlier, police struggled to contain the unruly postgame celebration.

"It got me excited when I saw Reggie do that, really pumped me up. I was 16 and had always been a Reds fan because we lived relatively close to Cincinnati, but that's when I first started thinking Yankees."

—Don Mattingly

# The Reggie Bar

Reggie Jackson had won three world titles with Oakland, but he craved a bigger stage for his slugging heroics, like New York City. "If I played there," he was quoted in *The Sporting News* in 1975, "they'd name a candy bar after me."

At the time, Baby Ruth and Oh Henry! were among America's favorite candy bars. Many assumed that the bars were named after Babe Ruth and Henry Aaron, who had surpassed the Babe as baseball's all-time home run king in 1974. The Ruth bar, which debuted in 1920, may have been named after the Yankees hero, although the Curtiss Candy Company denied it. Oh Henry!, also a Curtiss Candy product, was named after the bar's creator (Tom Henry) in 1919. In any case, since Baby Ruth and Oh Henry! existed, a Reggie bar seemed like a natural follow-up—especially after Jackson's five homers in the 1977 World Series.

The Curtiss Candy Company stepped to the plate, creating the Reggie bar in time for Opening Day 1978. Circular hunks of chocolate, peanuts, and caramel, the bars were handed to fans at the Yankees' home opener. That afternoon, both Jackson and the Yankees faithful responded in characteristic fashion. Jackson smashed a home run, and fans showered the field with empty wrappers.

# Nice Glove, Kid!

## October 9, 1996

Replays showed that Orioles outfielder Tony Tarasco had at least a chance at catching the ball and that the correct call probably should have been fan interference.

**Opposite Page:** In 1996, for the first time in Jeffrey Maier's life, the Yankees reached the American League Championship Series. Who would have guessed that he would determine the outcome?

Before Jeffrey Maier left with his dad for Yankee Stadium, he made sure to bring his baseball glove. After all, he would be sitting right behind the right-field fence. Wouldn't it be a dream to catch a home run ball, perhaps one hit by his idol, Yankees rookie Derek Jeter?

A 12-year-old from Old Tappan, New Jersey, Maier had received a ticket to this Wednesday afternoon contest as a bar mitzvah present. He couldn't have been more thrilled, for this was the Yankees' first American League Championship Series game in 15 years. The game was just as important for the Baltimore Orioles, who had endured a 13-year drought since making the playoffs. Game 1 was a nail-biter throughout, with Baltimore clinging to a 4-3 lead in the eighth inning. Little did Maier know that he himself would determine the outcome.

With the bases empty and one man out in the bottom of the eighth, Jeter lofted a high fly ball deep to right. Orioles right-fielder Tony Tarasco drifted way back, to the fence, and appeared to draw a bead on the ball—as did Maier. "The ballplayer in me just took over," he told the *Washington Post*. "I had never seen a ball hit that high before, but I was able to get to the spot. I had a pretty good idea of where it was going."

As the ball descended, Maier reached over the nine-foot-high wall. "It kind of hits the heel of my glove," he told the *Boston Globe*, "comes up into my chest, and rolls onto the floor." All eyes turned to right-field umpire Rich Garcia. Did the kid touch the ball after it had cleared the fence, making it a home run, or did he touch it in the field of play, meaning fan interference? Garcia didn't even hesitate. Home run, he signaled, and Yankee Stadium erupted in celebration. Jeter circled the bases with his first-ever postseason homer, assisted by his number one fan from Old Tappan, New Jersey.

Replays showed that Maier had indeed reached over the fence, and the Orioles protested vociferously. Tarasco insisted that he was about to catch the ball, and Orioles manager Davey Johnson demanded that Jeter be declared out, due to fan interference. But the umpires were unmoved, and the game proceeded. The Yankees went on to win 5-4 in the 11th inning on a Bernie Williams home run, but even then the Orioles wouldn't let it drop. They lodged an

official protest after the game. However, it was denied by AL President Gene Budig, because judgment calls could not be protested.

Over the next 24 hours (and beyond), Orioles fans turned their wrath toward the kid who they claimed cost them the game. Even sports columnist Tony Kornheiser of the *Washington Post* (whose readers were largely Orioles fans) was merciless toward the sixth-grader. He referred to Maier as "a truant," because he had skipped school to attend the game, and "a punk."

Meanwhile, Maier became an instant hero in New York and a celebrity nationwide. On Thursday morning, he appeared on both *Good Morning America* and *Live with Regis and Kathie Lee*, and later went on the *Late Show with David Letterman*. He became a media darling. "I didn't mean to do anything bad," he said at the time. "I'm just a 12-year-old kid trying to catch a ball." New York City Mayor Rudy Giuliani, a huge Yankees fan, gave Maier the Key to the City. Upper Deck even wanted to

Right-field umpire Rich Garcia gives Orioles manager Davey Johnson the thumb after Johnson vehemently protested Derek Jeter's home run. Johnson claimed that his outfielder, Tony Tarasco, would have caught the ball had Maier not gotten in the way.

While Derek Jeter (right) tied the game with his controversial homer, Bernie Williams (#51) won it with a solo shot in the bottom of the 11th. Although Baltimore bounced back with a win in Game 2, New York took the series in five.

publish a Jeffrey Maier baseball card, but his parents nixed the deal.

What followed, some say, is the Curse of Jeffrey Maier. The Yankees beat Baltimore in the ALCS four games to one, then won the World Series over Atlanta—their first of four world titles in a five-year stretch. The Orioles, meanwhile, would lose the ALCS again the next season, and then endure a decade of sub-.500 campaigns. "I could still be in Baltimore if that didn't happen," groused manager Davey Johnson, let go after the 1997 season, to the *Washington Post*. "It was a real big game, and we were going to win it.… It got me fired—not immediately, but it got me fired."

Maier, meanwhile, went on to have a normal childhood, except for a brief encounter with his hero in February 1997, when he met Jeter at a baseball card show. "He took a couple of minutes to privately meet me," Maier told the *Boston Globe*. "Being 12 and meeting your hero, I was somewhat speechless." But Jeter showed his appreciation. "He gave me his wristband," Maier said, "and he signed a ball, 'To Jeff, Thanks a lot, Derek Jeter.' I still have that. That was real cool."

# Maier an Oriole?

What was the best way for the Orioles to exorcise the Curse of Jeffrey Maier? In 2006, the team's owner thought about drafting Maier himself. The idea wasn't as preposterous as it seemed. Maier, it turned out, had developed into quite a ballplayer. In fact, he had become captain of the Wesleyan University baseball team and had even set the school record for career hits.

When informed of Maier's accomplish-ments by a *Washington Post* reporter, Orioles owner Peter Angelos mulled over the idea of selecting him in the 2006 amateur draft. "I was at that [1996] game," Angelos said, "and he certainly did seem to be a heck of an outfielder. Sure, we'd take him. In fact, I like the idea more and more, the more I think about it."

The Orioles scouting department thought otherwise. Though an exceptional line-drive hitter, Maier lacked size, speed, and power. He had also faced mediocre competition in college while playing for a Division III school. He ended up going undrafted.

Nevertheless, Maier captured people's attention again in recent years. In a game at Williams College in Massachusetts during his sophomore year, he attracted news coverage when Yankee-hating Red Sox fans threw ice chunks at him. Seeking a career in baseball, Maier has worked as a scout for ESPN's Peter Gammons and has interned with the YES Network, which broadcasts Yankee games.

Maier, it seems, doesn't mind the spotlight. While at Williams College, a fellow student (and Orioles fan) produced a short film entitled "I Hate Jeffrey Maier." The real-life antagonist agreed to make a cameo, in which he apologizes for causing so much anguish in Baltimore. It's doubtful that Orioles fans believed him—or forgave him.

# Yankees Gallop to Title

## October 26, 1996

Catcher Joe Girardi rose to the occasion in the Game 6 finale. The stocky catcher legged out a triple to knock in the first run and also gunned down two Atlanta baserunners.

**Opposite Page:** Determined to avoid post-championship chaos, the Yankees lined the field with New York's finest. Wade Boggs decided it would be fun to hitch a ride.

Yankee Stadium hardly looked the part of intimidating home-field advantage after the first two games of the 1996 World Series.

Following a rainout of the first game that was to have taken place on a Saturday, the Atlanta Braves crushed the Yankees in Game 1, 12-1, and then shut them out 4-0 in Game 2. As a result, the Braves effectively turned the grand old ballpark into what felt like a tomb for baseball legends of the past. And the local media buried them accordingly.

Then a funny thing happened when the Yankees went on the road. Playing National League rules in the National League ballpark in Atlanta, the Yankees reclaimed their dignity by sweeping the Braves to the tune of 5-2, 8-6, and 1-0. Holding a 3-2 Series advantage, the Yankees returned to Yankee Stadium for Game 6 with their 23rd World Series on the horizon. And they returned a different team, a team that now believed they would win.

No other stadium in sports could boast of having a home crowd like the one congregating in the Bronx. The Braves had removed that advantage in each of the first two games by taking early leads.

"Those first two games at home, we really didn't have anything going," Yankees outfielder Darryl Strawberry was quoted in the *Tampa Tribune*. "But we have something going now. And I think we'll show it.

"We've got a shot at winning a World Series now, and I think the whole city of New York is excited about that. People said we weren't going to show up [in Atlanta], but we showed up. Now, we're going home."

A different Yankee Stadium embraced the Yankees for Game 6 on October 26. Much of the enthusiasm stemmed from the emotional story of Yankees manager Joe Torre, who had sat on pins and needles the day before Game 6 while his brother, Frank, underwent a successful heart transplant. Torre had not been a popular choice to become the manager prior to the 1996 season, but he had proved to be the right choice. He knew how to manage a game and deftly handle the unique demands of Yankees owner George Steinbrenner.

The Yankees had not won a World Series since 1978, and the crowd sensed something

"From the time you start playing baseball, you think about playing in the World Series. It was the greatest feeling, no question. But I won't lie, you get a little spoiled because you expect to make it every year. There's so much tradition here."

—Derek Jeter

special about to happen. The cheers began at first glimpse of Yankees starter Jimmy Key—walking alongside pitching coach Mel Stottlemyre from the Yankees' dugout to the bullpen to warm up prior to the game—and they never stopped.

Seeing Key could not have been a confidence-booster for the Braves. The crafty left-hander had won the decisive Game 6 for the Toronto Blue Jays in the 1992 World Series against the Braves.

The clamor in Yankee Stadium intensified in the third inning, when Joe Girardi tripled home Paul O'Neill to put the Yankees up 1-0. The volume continued to rise when Derek Jeter's RBI single moved the lead to 2-0, and reached a crescendo when Bernie Williams' double put the Yankees up 3-0.

On defense, Girardi thwarted Braves rallies by throwing out runners in the third and fifth innings. Marquis Grissom became one of the victims in the fifth, and argued with umpire Terry Tata after the call. The enraged Braves center fielder had to be restrained during the argument, which ended with Braves manager Bobby Cox becoming the sixth manager in World Series history to be ejected from the game.

Yankees closer John Wetteland worked to retire Braves second baseman Mark Lemke, with two outs in the top of the ninth. Anticipating

"You haven't heard loudness until you've heard Yankee Stadium in October. People are so emotional and passionate and intense. To me, it's the greatest place to play."

—Joe Girardi

the outcome, New York policemen on horseback lined the perimeter of the field. Wetteland delivered, and Lemke popped up the pitch to Charlie Hayes; the Yankees third baseman made the catch for the final out to preserve a 3-2 Yankees win. Once again, the Yankees were the kings of baseball and a raucous party on the field followed. Amid the chaos, Wade Boggs hitched a ride with one of New York's finest—on horseback—and rode around Yankee Stadium, waving to the jubilant fans in one of the more unique celebrations in the history of sports.

Torre, who had experienced a whirlwind of emotions during his first season as manager of the Yankees, spoke through a champagne bath afterward.

"This is the best feeling, between yesterday and today, the best feeling of my life," the Yankees manager told the *Tampa Tribune*. "I never had my doubts about this club."

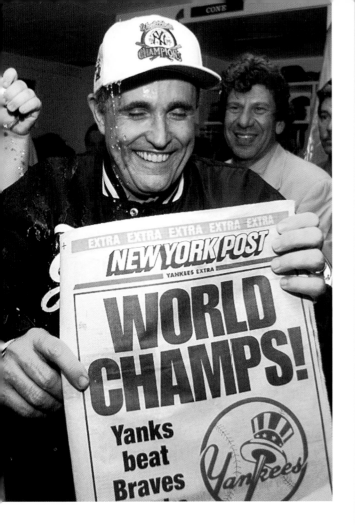

New York Mayor Rudolph Giuliani, who let everyone know that he rooted for the Yankees and not the Mets, celebrates the title.

**Opposite Page Left:** Andy Pettitte, who led the AL with 21 wins in 1996, hit the showers in the third inning of Game 1 but led New York to a 1-0 triumph in Game 5.

**Opposite Page Right:** Third baseman Charlie Hayes, a late-season acquisition from Pittsburgh, squeezes the final out of Game 6, clinching New York's first world title since 1978.

## Torre Wins 'Em Over

On November 2, 1995, the New York Yankees' announcement that Joe Torre would replace manager Buck Showalter evoked much grousing among veteran New York sportswriters and diehard baseball fans. In Torre's three prior managing stints with the New York Mets, Atlanta Braves, and St. Louis Cardinals, respectively, his teams had compiled a less-than-impressive record of 109 games under .500.

So the negative sentiment by some in the New York media was understandable. Showalter had led the team to the playoffs in 1995, and had there not been a strike in 1994, the Yankees would have made the playoffs then as well. However, one telling stat in Yankees lore bode well for Torre: the only manager to have a worse record prior to taking over as the Yankees' skipper was none other than legendary Casey Stengel.

Stengel brought in a managerial ledger that showed him 161 games under .500. Of course, under Stengel, the Yankees ruled the baseball world with a composite record of 1,149-696, which made Yankee Stadium the temple of doom for opposing teams.

Torre played 2,209 major-league games for the Milwaukee and Atlanta Braves, the Cardinals, and the Mets, and never made it to the World Series; nor had he done so as a manager when he took the Yankees job. However, like Stengel, Torre thrived as the Yankees manager, bringing calm to the team and serving as a buffer between the team's owner, George Steinbrenner, and the players. After winning the 1996 World Series, the Yankees went on to win three more world championships in the next four years. Not bad for a manager few thought should have the job.

# Yankees Restore New York Pride

## October 30 - November 1, 2001

With two outs in the bottom of the ninth of Game 4, Tino Martinez rocks D'Backs submariner Byung-Hyun Kim with a two-run homer, stunningly tying the game at 3-3.

**Opposite Page:** In what Joe Torre referred to as "Groundhog Day," Scott Brosius repeated Martinez's feat with a ninth-inning, two-out, two-run, game-tying homer in Game 5, also off Byung-Hyun Kim.

The New York Yankees were trailing the Arizona Diamondbacks two games to none in the 2001 World Series, but they were coming home to the Bronx to play the next three games at Yankee Stadium. After the Yankees won a hard-fought 2-1 victory in Game 3, Curt Schilling, who would be on the Yankee Stadium mound as Arizona's Game 4 starting pitcher, was asked to comment on the mystique and aura of Yankee Stadium, as evidenced by the team's unprecedented championship tradition.

"Mystique and aura," Schilling replied sarcastically, "those are dancers in a nightclub."

He couldn't have been farther off-base.

On October 31, 2001, Yankee Stadium hosted the first major-league game ever played on Halloween. Appropriately, the game had a bizarre finish. Schilling had stymied the Yankees for seven innings, and left the game with a two-run lead. Arizona's side-arming relief pitcher, Byung-Hyun Kim, entered the game to record the final six outs. He dispatched the Yankees quickly in the eighth, and, with two outs in the ninth inning, the Yankees were one out away from going down in the Series three games to one. Paul O'Neill was on first base and Tino Martinez, hitless in his previous 10 plate appearances, was in the batter's box. Kim seemed unhittable, and the Yankees needed a miracle. They got one.

On Kim's first pitch, Martinez swung and lashed a high-arcing line drive that carried over the right-center-field wall for a dramatic home run to tie the score. The stadium's upper tiers were rocking and the concrete floor was rolling. A fan's poster said it all that night: "We're Back." How true it was. Just weeks after the September 11 tragedy, New Yorkers were counting mightily on the Yankees to help restore the pride and spirit of their indomitable city. And now a critical game, so perilously close to being lost, had new life.

As the game went into extra innings, the stadium clock struck midnight. It was now November 1—the first time a World Series game had ever been played in November. The Yankees captain, Derek Jeter, fouled off three tough pitches from the South Korean reliever before running the count full. Then Jeter smacked Kim's next pitch toward the right-field

"The tragedy left us feeling so helpless, it felt good to touch people who needed something to hold on to. To me the most touching moment was in the Armory when Bernie [Williams] went up to one woman and said, 'I don't know what to say, but you look like you need a hug,' and he hugged her."

—Joe Torre

corner. The ball snuck inside the foul pole and landed in the first row of seats for a game-winning home run to even the Series at two games apiece. The crowd erupted with a primordial scream lasting several minutes, as Jeter trotted around the bases, his right fist raised in the air, before jumping onto home plate and into the waiting arms of his jubilant teammates.

The gravity of the moment was not lost on Jeter.

"I've never hit a walk-off homer," said the Yankees' new Mr. November. "I don't think I hit one in Little League. That was huge."

The next night, in Game 5, Arizona again held a two-run lead in the ninth inning, and once more, manager Bob Brenly called on Kim to protect it. Jorge Posada was on second base with two outs,

and the Yankees were again down to their last out, just as they were when Martinez tied Game 4 with a homer off Kim. This time, Scott Brosius played the hero, connecting on Kim's second pitch and propelling the ball deep beyond the left-field wall. It was the second time in as many nights that the Yankees had come back from the brink of defeat by hitting a two-run home run with two outs in the ninth to tie the game.

"It's Groundhog Day," said Joe Torre. "This is the most incredible couple of games I've ever managed." As Brosius began to celebrate his two-run homer, the rampant emotion throughout the stadium crackled like lightning; the buzzing didn't stop until the smoke had cleared in the 12th inning, when Alfonso Soriano singled home Chuck Knoblauch with the winning run for a 3-2 Yankees Series lead.

A fan sitting behind the Arizona dugout unfurled a banner that proclaimed, "Mystique and aura appearing nightly." The Yankees had done it again, and now led the Series three games to two. While the Diamondbacks rebounded to win the final two games at Arizona, 15-2 and 3-2, the Yankees' inspired play made for one of the most memorable Series in baseball history.

"People were pulling for us, it was pretty impressive. Everywhere we went, people said they were hoping we'd win it for the city of New York. We represented more than the Yankees—we represented the firefighters, the rescue workers, the whole city."

—Derek Jeter

In the first major event staged in New York after 9/11, the World Series went on as scheduled—albeit amid intense security.

Derek Jeter leaps into his teammates' arms at home plate after his emotional walk-off homer in the 10th inning of Game 4. Since the game ended after midnight on Halloween night, Jeter earned the nickname "Mr. November."

# Bush's First Pitch

The national mourning in the aftermath of the September 11 terrorist attacks had resulted in the extension of that year's baseball season, so Game 3 of the 2001 World Series, played on October 30, marked the latest date that a major-league game had ever been contested.

Moments before game time, a tall right-hander from Texas popped out of the Yankees dugout and began striding toward the pitcher's mound to thunderous applause from the 55,820 fans cheering "USA! USA!" George W. Bush, the 43rd president of the United States, waved to the New York crowd, and toed the Yankee Stadium pitcher's slab.

For the first time in 45 years, a sitting president would throw out the ceremonial first pitch at a World Series game. Only four other presidents had ever thrown out the ceremonial first pitch at a World Series game while still serving in office. And none had made a fall classic pitch since Dwight Eisenhower did, before the opening game of the 1956 Series at Ebbets Field in Brooklyn.

Security at a World Series game had never been more paramount than it was for President Bush's appearance at Yankee Stadium, following the terrorist attacks. Though no one realized it at the time, there was an extra umpire on the field for the pregame ceremony who turned out to be a Secret Service agent working undercover.

As the president reared back into his throwing motion, stretching his sweatshirt emblazoned with "FDNY," a tribute to the New York City Fire Department, the outline of a bulletproof vest became visible. Seemingly unencumbered, the president fired a strike to the Yankee backup catcher, Todd Greene. Suddenly, a convoy of air force military jets flying in a V-formation screamed over the stadium light stanchions. Then the other marquee Texan, Roger Clemens, took the mound for the Yankees and overpowered the Diamondbacks with his fastball and sinker.

# Boone Prolongs the Curse

## October 16, 2006

Red Sox ace Pedro Martinez had a comfortable 5-2 lead in the eighth inning of Game 7 before surrendering a single and three doubles. The game entered extra innings tied 5-5.

**Opposite Page:** Aaron Boone goes deep off knuckleballer Tim Wakefield in the 11th inning of Game 7 of the 2003 ALCS. Thereafter, Boone joined Bucky Dent among the most cursed names in Beantown.

Though he hails from big-league bloodlines, Aaron Boone might be the least likely hero among the many who have played that role in Yankees pinstripes. He certainly did not fill out his jersey with the muscle of past Bronx greats, or any of his heavy-hitting 2003 teammates, for that matter. Boone had been traded from Cincinnati in July of that year to fill a New York void at third base. He had done so admirably, if unspectacularly, batting .254 in 54 games, but now he was in the midst of a miserable playoff debut.

Boone hit just .200 in the 2003 American League Division Series, which the Yankees won over the Twins. In the first six games of a tense, fight-marred American League Championship Series against rival Boston, Boone had mustered only two hits in 16 at-bats, and neither of those singles left the infield. The resulting .125 average had him on Joe Torre's bench to start the seventh and final game at Yankee Stadium.

No one could have predicted that Red Sox fans would soon be muttering Boone's name along with those of Bucky (Bleeping) Dent and Bill (Bleeping) Buckner, in the long line of players who had helped prolong the "Curse of the Bambino": the hex that had supposedly kept Boston from claiming a World Series title since 1918. After Boone went hitless in Game 6 in the series, his big brother Bret, reported *USA Today* columnist Ian O'Connor, told Aaron, "Hey, you stink right now.… Do something tomorrow and everyone will forget all about that."

Very little was forgettable about this ALCS. The most indelible image before Boone took center stage was that of 72-year-old Yankees coach Don Zimmer, appearing poised to try a punch, charging Boston's Pedro Martinez at Fenway Park in Game 3, and being shoved to the ground by the Red Sox ace. It was the defining moment of a bench-clearing episode that followed questionable pitches by both Martinez and Yankee Roger Clemens, a hard slide into second base by New York's Karim Garcia, and verbal barbs by players from both teams throughout the contest.

"I think when the series began," Red Sox manager Grady Little told the *Boston Globe* after the Yankees' 4-3 victory gave them a 2-1 edge in the series, "everyone knew it was

going to be quite a battle, it was going to be very emotional, there was going to be a lot of intensity. But I think we've upgraded it from a battle to a war."

Zimmer was transported by ambulance to a hospital for tests after the ordeal, but was not seriously injured. Back at Fenway, the night grew even uglier in the ninth inning, when a member of the grounds crew scuffled with New York reliever Jeff Nelson in the bullpen. Ill will between these longtime rivals appeared to be reaching a new high—or perhaps new low, in this case. Given their history, that was some achievement.

The Red Sox relied on their knuckleballer instead of their knuckles in Game 4, as Tim Wakefield twirled his second win of the series, 3-2, to square the set at two games apiece. The Yankees' 4-2 victory the next day put them on the brink of the World Series as they wrapped up the memorable Fenway portion of the ALCS. Their celebration was put on hold, however,

"I don't know if I believe in curses, or jinxes, or anything like that. But I'll tell you what I do believe—I believe in ghosts. And we've got some ghosts in this stadium."

—Derek Jeter

103

The long-simmering Red Sox-Yankees rivalry culminated in a bench-clearing brawl in Game 3, in which Pedro Martinez shoved 72-year-old Yankee's coach Don Zimmer (pictured) to the ground.

Hideki Matsui jumps for joy after scoring the tying run in the eighth inning of Game 7. He and Bernie Williams scored on a house-rocking double by Jorge Posada.

**Opposite Page:** Before Boone reached second base during his home run trot, Mariano Rivera had reached the mound for his own personal celebration. Rivera (1-0, two saves) was named series MVP.

when Boston came roaring back from a 6-4 deficit with three runs in the seventh inning at Yankee Stadium in Game 6, winning 9-6 and stretching the series to its limit.

For most of Game 7, it seemed Boone would not get a chance to take up his brother's challenge. He had been benched in favor of Enrique Wilson at third base. Few, if any, of the 56,279 packed into Yankee Stadium seemed to pay much attention to that move. All eyes on October 16, 2003, were on the pitching matchup between Martinez and Clemens, an anticipated rematch of their Game 3 staredown.

That matchup went Martinez's way early on. Firing heat, he kept the Yankees off the scoreboard and quieted, at least to an extent, their fans through the first four innings. Meanwhile, Boston's bats came up with four runs in those frames, chasing Clemens with no outs in the fourth. Mike Mussina got the call for his first career relief appearance, and threw three shutout innings as New York inched closer, scoring runs in the fifth and seventh on solo homers by Jason Giambi.

The Red Sox should have taken a lesson from the Yankees' relief success. A tiring Martinez took a 5-2 lead into the bottom of the eighth inning, but Little decided to stick with his ace, even after Derek Jeter doubled, Bernie Williams singled, and the

Boston manager made a visit to the mound. Doubles by Hideki Matsui and Jorge Posada followed, and the Yankees had tied the game, 5-5.

Boone, who had been inserted as a pinch runner in the eighth and stayed in to play third base through two scoreless innings and the clock striking midnight, wondered if he might be lifted in the 11th, when he was scheduled to lead off. Wakefield was on the hill, and Boone had done nothing against his knuckleball in two previous games in the series. Torre gave him one more chance, and Boone used it to make history.

The first pitch came fluttering toward him—a knuckler, as Boone had predicted. He put a no-doubt swing on it, and the ball went soaring toward the left-field seats. Up in the TV booth, a tear began to well up in his brother's eye before the sphere reached the screaming fans. "That's as big as it gets right there," Bret told a Fox television audience in his analyst's role.

Meanwhile, his younger brother took a break from celebrating his newfound heroism in the clubhouse to say, "When I joined the Yankees, this is the kind of thing I wanted to be part of."

The Yankees were once again American League champions, winning the game 6-5, and the series 4-3. The Red Sox would have to wait another year to exorcise the Curse of the Bambino

"To be honest, I really didn't enjoy playing the Red Sox, we were so evenly matched. Every game—and we played them 26 times—was a huge struggle. What made this so sweet was coming from behind—our guys never quit. Booney was a guy really struggling, so seeing him hit that big home run was very special."

—Joe Torre

# Bad Blood

Of course, the bad blood between the Yankees and Red Sox began long before their 2003 American League Championship Series meeting. Here's a look at their most heated moments through the years at Yankee Stadium.

**May 30, 1938:** Jake Powell of the Yankees charges the mound after being beaned in the stomach by Archie McKain. Boston shortstop Joe Cronin, known for his temper, races to his pitcher's defense and engages Powell in the middle of the diamond. The players trade punches for several minutes before a crowd of 85,533, the largest ever at Yankee Stadium. Both men are ejected, but resume their fight under the stands, with some saying Powell got the better of it. Each is suspended 10 games.

**June 21, 1967:** New York's Thad Tillotson hits Joe Foy in the head with a pitch, prompting Boston's Jim Lonborg to plunk Tillotson in the shoulder when he comes to bat. The two pitchers exchange words, Foy runs across the field to challenge Tillotson to a fight, and both benches clear. With Joe Pepitone leading the Yankees into battle and Rico Petrocelli on the Red Sox front line, players scuffle.

**May 20, 1976:** A battle of bruisers takes shape, when Lou Piniella chugs toward home plate and crashes into Red Sox catcher Carlton Fisk, feet first, while being tagged out. The two become entwined and begin swinging as they climb to their feet. The dugouts empty and an ugly scrap follows. From his spot on second base, Graig Nettles tackles Boston pitcher Bill Lee. Lee injures his shoulder in a pileup. Things deteriorate further when objects are thrown from the stands, prompting Boston's Don Zimmer to wear a helmet to the third-base coach's box.

**September 13, 1986:** About 25 members of the Red Sox climb into the left-field stands at Yankee Stadium, after a Brooklyn fan snatches outfielder Jim Rice's cap. No reports of fighting or injuries.

**September 18, 1993:** The Red Sox are livid following an incident in the bottom of the ninth at Yankee Stadium. New York batter Mike Stanley appears to end the game with a flyout, but an ump calls time just before the pitch because a Yankee fan ran onto the field. The Yanks then rally to win, 4-3.

# Part 3

# *Stadium Milestones*

# Ruth Christens Yankee Stadium

## April 18, 1923

This postcard illustrates the original Yankee Stadium design (inset) as well as the finished product, as pictured in the ballpark's inaugural season, 1923.

**Opposite Page:** Babe Ruth immediately found Yankee Stadium's short right-field porch to his liking, belting one over the barrier in his first at-bat ever in the new ballpark.

On January 3, 1920, the New York Yankees purchased George Herman Ruth's contract from the Boston Red Sox. They shelled out $125,000 for Ruth, along with a loan for $300,000 against the mortgage on Fenway Park. In return, they got a slugger who rewrote the record books, lured fans to the ballpark by the thousands, and led the Bronx Bombers to seven pennants and four World Series championships.

Thirteen months later, on February 6, 1921, the Yankees spent even more for a plot of land—specifically, 10 acres on the west side of the Bronx. They paid $675,000 to the estate of William Waldorf Astor for the earth that would become their new ballpark. Now that the Yankees had baseball's marquee attraction on their roster, they decided that the Polo Grounds, which they shared with the Giants, was too small a home. The top architects were put on the task of designing a modern marvel of a park, and in 1922, a New York construction company was given a $2.5 million budget and 11 months to finish Yankee Stadium.

Remarkably, it took 284 working days, just enough time to unveil Yankee Stadium for Opening Day 1923. It was a colossal composition of wood, concrete, and steel—the most expansive and expensive stadium of its day. Beamed F. C. Lane in the May 1923 edition of *Literary Digest*, "The Yankee Stadium is indeed the last word in ballparks. But not the least of its merits is its advantage of position. From the plain of the Harlem River it looms up like the great Pyramid of Cheops from the sands of Egypt."

Yet for all the toil that went into erecting a cathedral that would become the standard by which major-league stadiums would be judged, it took Ruth exactly one swing of the bat to put his legendary stamp on the House That Ruth Built. The christening took place on April 18, 1923.

Opening Day is always thrilling for baseball fans. This particular Opening Day was one of a kind for New Yorkers. Their Yankees were coming off back-to-back American League flags, the first in their history. They had baseball's best player in Ruth. And now, they had the best stadium—a park built to hold 58,000, but one which swelled with thousands more on this day. The attendance was announced at more than 74,200, though that figure was exaggerated. Thousands more were turned away by the fire department. As Geoffrey Ward and Ken Burns report in *Baseball*, "The heads were packed in so closely that Al Goullet, the six-day bicycle rider, could have ridden his bike around the stadium on the track of their hats."

The governor, mayor, and police chief, along with Commissioner Kenesaw Mountain Landis, were among those in the stands. Even those who were unable to get inside could hear John Phillip Sousa and the Seventh Regiment Band play, as the club raised its team flag and the 1922 pennant in center field. Ruth was given a glass-enclosed bat during the opening ceremonies.

Days earlier, Ruth was said to have been hitting balls in the snow, trying to belt one into the outfield seats at the ornate new ballpark. *The*

*New York Times* reported that the Babe "swatting several drives over the billowing snow ... didn't come anywhere near the fences."

This was his afternoon, however. Ruth, always the center of attention, had told reporters before the game that he would give a year of his life if he could hit a home run in the first game at Yankee Stadium. "The Babe was on trial," stated *The New York Times*, "and he knew it better than anybody else."

Opposing the Yankees was their rival, the Red Sox. Life had not been good for Boston since selling Ruth to New York. The Red Sox had finished with the worst record in the American League the previous season, winning less than 40 percent of their games. Frank Chance, the former Cubs player/manager, took over for the 1923 campaign, debuting in Yankee Stadium's opener.

Chance chose Howard Ehmke as his starting pitcher. Ehmke had won 17 games in 1922 and would claim 20 wins in '23. This would not be one of them. Ruth's flair for the dramatic had already been well-established. Why should this day, against this pitcher, be different?

It did not take long for Ruth to work his magic. Yankee Stadium shook when he stepped to the plate in the bottom half of the first inning, with two runners already having reached base. "The ball came in slowly," depicted *The New York Times* in its recounting of the moment, "but it went out quite rapidly, rising on a line and then dipping suddenly from the force behind it. It struck well inside the foul line, eight or ten rows above the low railing in the front of the bleachers, and as Ruth circled the bases he received probably the greatest ovation of his career. The biggest crowd rose to its feet and let loose the loudest shout in baseball history. Ruth, jogging over the home plate, grinned broadly, lifted his cap at arm's length, and waved it to the multitude."

The three-run blast was the difference in the Yankees' 4-1 win against the Red Sox. It was

also a precursor of things to come. Ruth led the American League in homers, runs, RBI, walks, slugging, and on-base percentage that season, and won his only Most Valuable Player award. He led the Yankees to a third straight pennant, and this time—with this grand ballpark as the setting—they completed their mission by winning the World Series for the first time in their history.

Some were more awed by the setting than the slugger. "Foolish stories have floated about that the playingfield was designedly limited so as to enable Babe Ruth to break his home run record," Lane wrote in *Literary Digest*. "One needs but to glance at these stories to see their falsity. Babe Ruth is at the best a temporary attraction. A few seasons at the most and his great feats will be but a memory. The Yankee Stadium, however, is a permanent institution."

The House That Ruth Built, indeed.

**Opposite Page Left:** Police officers and dignitaries honor America during Opening Day ceremonies. New York Governor Al Smith, New York Mayor John Hylan, and MLB Commissioner Kenesaw Mountain Landis joined the festivities.

**Opposite Page Right:** Fans flock to Yankee Stadium on April 18, 1923, for the first game ever at the spectacular baseball palace. Reportedly, 74,200 fans attended the historic event.

# Yankee Stadium "Firsts"

Babe Ruth's first-inning home run was the most memorable of many "firsts" in Yankee Stadium. Most of those milestones, like Ruth's, took place on April 18, 1923, as the Yankees hosted Boston. Other "firsts" soon followed in the first ballpark to be named "stadium," rather than "grounds," "park," or "field." A sampling (with date in parentheses for games other than the April 18, 1923, opener) of those notables:

- First game: Yankees 4, Red Sox 1
- First pitch: Bob Shawkey, New York (ball one)
- First batter: Chick Fewster, Boston (grounded out)
- First hit: George Burns, Boston (single)
- First Yankees batter: Whitey Witt
- First Yankees hit: Aaron Ward
- First RBI: Joe Dugan, New York
- First stolen base: Joe Harris and George Burns, Boston (double-steal, April 19, 1923)
- First double: Bob Meusel, New York
- First triple: Norm McMillan, Boston
- First home run: Babe Ruth, New York
- First grand slam: Tris Speaker, Cleveland (June 9, 1923)
- First inside-the-park homer: Sam Rice, Washington (April 25, 1923)
- First sacrifice hit: Everett Scott, New York
- First sacrifice fly: Dugan (April 21, 1923)
- First cycle: Goose Goslin, Washington (August 28, 1924)
- First hit batsman: Fewster (by Shawkey)
- First pitching win: Shawkey
- First pitching loss: Howard Ehmke, Boston
- First shutout: Sam Jones, New York (4-0 vs. Washington, April 24, 1923)
- First no-hitter: Monte Pearson, New York (13-0 vs. Cleveland, August 27, 1938)

# Night Ball in the Bronx

## May 28, 1946

Yankees President Larry MacPhail celebrates with manager Bucky Harris after the 1947 World Series. MacPhail brought lights to Major League Baseball in 1935 and to Yankee Stadium in 1946.

**Opposite Page:** Nearly 50,000 fans pack Yankee Stadium for the park's first night game, staged on a Tuesday night. For the first time, fans faced the reality of getting up early for work after a late night at the ballyard.

When World War II ended, the national pastime was eager to get back in full swing. The players-turned-soldiers had returned. Fans who had stayed away from ballparks in droves during the war years were also eager to return.

And new Yankees president Leland Stanford (Larry) MacPhail, a progressive and blustery man, was brimming with ideas for postwar consumerism. MacPhail, who along with partners Del Webb and Dan Topping had purchased the Yankees in 1945 for a bargain $2.8 million from the Jacob Ruppert estate (the original cost was $3 million), was a brilliant innovator.

In previous regimes in Cincinnati and Brooklyn, MacPhail had pioneered the use of batting helmets, presented the first televised game, and initiated night baseball in 1935, a radical break of baseball tradition. Despite the novelty resulting in an increase in attendance, not all teams enthusiastically switched over. It was too major an investment. It wasn't traditional. Later, the threat of war created paranoia, with lighted ballparks seen as easy targets for enemy planes.

Ed Barrow, the Yankees' top executive at the time, was one of the staunchest opponents of night baseball. "A team which can draw without night baseball is a sucker to go for lights," Barrow told *The Sporting News* in 1940. "You can't make me believe that the kind of play you see under the lights, with its shadows and its exaggerations, is real baseball.

"Still there are thousands of fans … willing to go for night ball. I admit that in a big city like New York there are thousands of workers who cannot get off during the day, enough folks who want it to devote their weekends to golf or their friends; to establish a clientele for night baseball. However, I am afraid that the game under lights might turn out to be a passing fancy. It would be tough to invest $250,000 in lights and then discover the fad had passed and you are stuck with a white elephant."

Barrow, a conservative man who ran the Yankees in a dictatorial style, never altered his reasoning. But when MacPhail came to power with the sale of the team, Yankee Stadium would be altered forever. Before the 1946 season, he spent $600,000 to renovate the ballpark.

"I came up the last two weeks of that season, every game in the afternoon. The next few years it seemed every Friday night was a night game. Played about 14 or15 night games a year then. It was still kind of new and the crowds were enthusiastic. It was fun."

—Yogi Berra

"I always enjoyed playing at night; the lights at the stadium were truly magnificent and bright. As a pitcher, I actually preferred day games. We got those shadows from the top tier, which became a tool for the pitcher. They'd creep around home plate and it was harder for the batter to see."

—Mel Stottlemyre

The Yankees' first night game happened to be Bill Dickey's managerial debut. Dickey was expected to outperform just-fired Joe McCarthy, whose .615 career winning percentage is the greatest in history.

Fans pack every inch of the Stadium for a 1947 World Series game. The Bombers drew a million fans for the first time in '46 and averaged more than 72,000 in the '47 Series.

And as he did in Crosley and Ebbets Fields, with positive results, he installed arc lights atop the House That Ruth Built. MacPhail boasted that the lights would provide illumination the equivalent of 5,000 full moons.

Ever the showman, MacPhail introduced night baseball at Yankee Stadium with a flourish. On the chilly night of May 28, 1946, the Yankees played the Washington Senators in former star catcher Bill Dickey's managerial debut. MacPhail had just fired legendary skipper Joe McCarthy, as the Yankees would go through three managers that season.

MacPhail brought in a 150-piece marching band and hired Metropolitan Opera soprano Rose Bampton to belt out the national anthem. Before a crowd of 49,917 on a dreary weekday night, General Electric president Charles Wilson pulled the switch, unveiling an amazing radiance (1,245 floodlights) that was twice as bright as any other outdoor sporting venue. "In fact," noted *The New York Times*, "the installation generates sufficient light to illuminate a four-lane highway from New York to Washington."

Though the Yankees lost the game, 2-1, on Washington knuckleballer Dutch Leonard's six-hitter, a new era had dawned with the newer, brighter stadium. As historian Leonard Koppett wrote of the postwar acceptance of night games, "It moved baseball across the imperceptible line between 'sport' and 'entertainment,' pushing the business into competition with other businesses in ways it had not been forced to confront before, especially movies and television."

The Yankees would go on to draw a record 2,265,512 customers during the 1946 season—the first time they drew over one million fans since 1930. Without question, the introduction of night baseball at the stadium—the 13th of 16 ballparks to install lights—was a huge attendance impetus. Some 683,744 fans witnessed the 14 night games played in '46. That the national pastime is now mostly a nighttime pastime is part of the genius that was Larry MacPhail.

# Barrow-minded Tradition

Ed Barrow, the general manager when the House That Ruth Built opened in 1923, was a harsh critic of night baseball. He also had little use for Larry MacPhail.

Before MacPhail came to the Bronx, Barrow was the man most responsible for making the Yankees the mightiest team in sports. He was a shrewd judge of talent, originally known for discovering a coal miner's son named Honus Wagner. Years later, he convinced Babe Ruth to switch from pitching to hitting.

Barrow was a tight-fisted executive with menacing eyebrows. He knew baseball, knew the business side of it, and along with his protégé (and successor) George Weiss, emphasized scouting and development and made the Yankees' farm system tops in the game.

But Barrow never saw the light when it came to night baseball. "I am more convinced than ever," he said in the 1930s, "that there is absolutely no future in electric lighted play." And he didn't change his opinion a decade later, even when most teams installed lights. "It's a wart on the nose of the game," he scoffed.

After Jacob Ruppert's heirs sold the team in 1945, Barrow was named the Yankees' chairman of the board. But there was too much friction with part-owner and president MacPhail, so Barrow resigned after the 1946 season.

His legacy included 14 pennants and 10 world championships. Eight years after he left, the Yankees dedicated a plaque to Barrow, which first hung on the center-field wall at the stadium, near the flagpole and the monuments to Ruth, Lou Gehrig, and Miller Huggins, and later in Monument Park. Edward Barrow's plaque reads, "Molder of a tradition of victory."

# The Stadium Gets a Facelift

## April 15, 1976

The city funded the renovation of not just the stadium but also its surroundings. Located in the crime-ridden Bronx, the area needed to appear clean and safe in order to attract fans.

**Opposite Page:** Yankees announcer Phil Rizzuto stands amid construction equipment on December 17, 1974. Though workers needed only 11 months to build Yankee Stadium, the renovation took more than two years.

Somehow, it seemed fitting that the newly renovated Yankee Stadium opened on Tax Day during America's Bicentennial year. That afternoon, more than 54,000 fans came to watch the national pastime while grousing about how much it cost. Grumbled one fan that day to a *New York Times* reporter, "It's the House That Ruth Built and the taxpayers were ripped off for."

Some fans groaned about the increased ticket prices. Box seats, formerly $4.50, were now a whopping $5.50. But most of the complaints were about the $100 million in tax money that was spent to refurbish the stadium and the immediate area. At the time, however, no one realized how much happiness that money would buy.

Just four years earlier, in 1972, the Yankees had been a franchise in disgrace. They hadn't contended in eight years and were drawing only 12,000 fans a game. The Mets, who had captured the hearts of the city with their world title in 1969, were attracting more than twice as many fans. Even Yogi Berra had changed sides, serving as Mets coach starting in 1965 before becoming their manager from 1972 to '75.

Yankee Stadium hadn't undergone a major renovation since it was built in 1923. Moreover, the surrounding area was so crime-ridden that only the toughest New Yorkers were willing to attend games. Even when they hosted Boston on September 13, 1972, in which a victory would have put them in first place, they drew only 15,000 fans. Wrote Larry Merchant of the *New York Post*, "The Yankees gave a party last night at the Stadium and almost nobody came."

CBS owned the Yankees, but in 1972 they were ready to dump them. One potential buyer, Herman Franks, wanted to move the team to the Meadowlands in New Jersey. Eventually, a group led by George Steinbrenner purchased the club for a paltry $10 million (about 1 percent of its current value). As part of the package, New York City agreed to the major renovation project.

While workers overhauled the stadium, the Yankees endured the indignity of playing their 1974 and '75 home games at the Mets' Shea Stadium. Instead of Joe DiMaggio gracing

center field in front of Babe Ruth's monument, Elliott Maddox sloshed on Shea's soggy turf. "[T]he outfield there didn't drain at all," Maddox said. "If it rained on Monday, it would still be wet the following Saturday. We had to put our feet in Baggies before putting on our spikes, just to keep our feet dry."

Back in the Bronx, the renovation continued. Workers replaced the stadium's copper facade with a replica. Outside, they added escalator towers next to the stadium's three entrances. Inside, workers removed 118 obstructive steel columns. The upper decks were cantilevered over the lower deck, improving sight lines for fans. Most noticeably, they replaced the old wooden seats with wider, plastic ones. The renovated park accommodated fewer fans, but nearly every seat was a good one. To dazzle young fans, the team also installed a 560-foot-long "telescreen." It wasn't color, but it did come in "nine shades of gray."

Although the scoreboard wasn't yet working on Opening Day, 1976, most fans praised the look of the renovated park. The color of the seats matched that of the sky above, creating a cheerful atmosphere. "The aisles are too skinny but the seats are nice," Bronx student John Panzarino

"Well, times change. Look what has happened today, they get 53,000 a game now in the new park. The old stadium, geez, sometimes we couldn't wait to go on a road trip, especially right-handed hitters like me. Sometimes I wish I could've played in the new stadium, too."

—Moose Skowron

The Yankees brought out the heavyweights for the Opening Day ceremony. Standing among Yogi Berra, Mickey Mantle, and Joe DiMaggio is Joe Louis, who had defeated Max Schmeling at the stadium in 1938.

A week before its reopening in 1976, Yankee Stadium is not quite ready for Opening Day. Patrons could get through the door for a couple bucks, while $5.50 got them a box seat.

told the *Times*. "It'll all be worth the money if the Yankees have a good year."

Panzarino didn't realize how right he was. The new digs attracted 2,012,434 fans in 1976—tops in the American League—and the big crowds inspired the Yankees to success. Chris Chambliss' walk-off homer in Game 5 of the 1976 ALCS shot New York to the World Series for the first time in 12 years. Moreover, the influx of ticket revenue allowed Steinbrenner to purchase free-agent superstars like Reggie Jackson, who led the Bombers to world championships in 1977 and '78.

Taxpayer money had not only renovated the stadium; it resurrected the franchise. The Yankees were back where they belonged—the preeminent franchise in all of Major League Baseball.

# The Renovation

Installed wider, plastic seats. Removed obstructive steel columns. Cantilevered upper deck for better sight lines. Increased slope of lower deck seats for better view. Lowered the field of play. Replaced copper façade with a replica. Installed 560-foot-long telescreen.

Stadium closed: 1974 and '75

Reopened: April 15, 1976

Architect: Praeger-Kavanaugh-Waterbury

Cost: $48 million

New capacity: 54,028 (old: 65,010)

New cost of box seat: $5.50

New cost of bleacher seat: $1.50

Left field: 312' (old: 301')
Left center: 430' (old: 457')
Center field: 417' (old: 463')
Right center: 385' (old: 407')
Right field: 310' (old: 296')

"I was playing at Shea when the stadium was being renovated, and didn't play there after it was renovated. It's a beautiful ballpark but some of that uniqueness of the old stadium was gone. It really played a lot different. You missed those massive canyons in right-center and left-center. I guess one good thing was they did away with those low fences. I remember specifically Frank Robinson diving against the wall and falling over for a game-saving catch against us in 1966—you miss that now."

—Mel Stottlemyre

# Four Million Strong

## September 24, 2005

The Yankees broke the AL attendance record in 2005.

**Opposite Page:** Beginning on Opening Night against Boston (pictured), the Yankees surpassed 50,000 in attendance 54 times in 2005, with a high of 55,327 against the Mets.

"No one goes there anymore," Yogi Berra once said. "It's too crowded."

When he cracked that famous Berraism decades ago, Yogi was speaking about a trendy restaurant. But in 2005, he could have been discussing Yankee Stadium. The average per-game attendance that year exceeded 50,000, and it was seemingly impossible to get a ticket. On September 24, for the second-to-last game of the season, the Bombers surpassed four million in attendance for the first time ever. The Yankees became only the third major-league team to record a quadruple million, joining the Colorado Rockies (1993) and Toronto Blue Jays (1992 and '93).

"It's an incredible achievement," beamed Yankees owner George Steinbrenner, "particularly when I remember that when I bought the Yankees, we had trouble drawing one million to the Stadium. We have the greatest fans in the world.... And I thank everyone in our organization, on and off the field, for helping to reach this amazing milestone."

The next day against Toronto, the Yankees drew 55,136 to finish with a season attendance of 4,090,696. The Yankees that afternoon not only beat the Blue Jays, 8-4, in a pivotal stretch-run game, but they also smashed Toronto's American League single-season attendance record.

But Steinbrenner still wasn't satisfied. Determined to pack as many fannies in the seats as possible in 2006, he pumped big bucks into the team's preseason direct-marketing campaign. The Yankees mailed their *Pride, Power, Pinstripes* ticket-information and fan-guide booklet to one million households. The 32-page publication, four pages longer than the previous season's, featured an ad offering game-used baseballs and bases to ticket buyers.

The 2006 Yankees won just two more games than in '05 (97 to 95), but they again smashed their own (and the AL's) season attendance record. Exactly 4,248,067 fans spun through the turnstiles. After May 26, the Yankees hosted more than 50,000 fans in every game for the duration of the season.

The attendance figures were startling, considering the prohibitive cost of tickets and concessions. Craig Digilio of New Paltz, New York, remembers going to Yankees games

"As a 17-year-old I got sponsored by my town of Sumter, South Carolina—place of 12,000 people—to go to New York. I took a cab from the Hotel New Yorker, passed all these skyscrapers and apartment buildings on the way to Yankee Stadium. I'll always remember walking out of the dugout, seeing this gigantic stadium, thinking, *This is unbelievable*."

—Bobby Richardson

New Yorkers spin through the turnstiles on September 23, 2005, a day before the Yankees became the third franchise ever to reach four million in attendance.

New York Governor George Pataki speaks during a groundbreaking ceremony for the new Yankee Stadium, scheduled to be completed in time for the 2009 season.

in 1957 when, "for a couple of bucks, you'd have a pretty decent seat in the infield." But 50 years later, "You can easily spend $100 a person," said Mike Signorelli, a resident of Highland, New York.

In 2007, the Yankees offered 17 varieties of ticket prices. The 10 most expensive—ranging from Field Championship ($300 if purchased in advance) to Loge Box MVP ($73)—quickly sold out for every game. Only three of the 17 types of tickets were under $50: Tier Box ($40), Tier Reserved ($19), and Bleachers ($12). Toss in the cost of transportation, food, and souvenirs ($25 for a yearbook; the same for a cap), and you're soon out $100 or more.

For years now, New Yorkers have grumbled about the high prices at the stadium. Michael Caracciolo, on his website The Kid from Brooklyn, says it's nothing short of robbery.

"What about the working man, the common working man!" he pleads to Steinbrenner in his online video.

And yet, despite consistently high attendance rates—and the most lucrative cable pact in baseball—the Yankees have still struggled to make ends meet. In fact, if the team fails to make or win the World Series, Steinbrenner takes a wallop to his pocketbook. According to the *New York Daily News*, the Yankees lost between $50 million and $85 million in 2005, when they fell to Anaheim in the ALDS. The reason they lost so much dough was their astronomical player payroll, which exceeded $200 million in '05. In addition, the Yankees had to pay a $34 million luxury tax. According to the rules of Major League Baseball, if a team's payroll exceeds a certain amount ($128 million in 2005), it is taxed on the excess. This taxed money is distributed to small-market teams that don't

"Being a rookie, and playing in front of a full house, 66,000 fans, in the [1964] World Series was tremendously exciting. Of course things went downhill in the next 10 years and the attendance falloff was severe—all those empty seats, depressing. You truly appreciate the experience of a jam-packed ballpark. In those championship years, the energy and electricity of Yankee Stadium was indescribable."

—Mel Stottlemyre

## Yankee Stadium Attendance

|      | Total      | AL Rank | Average |
|------|------------|---------|---------|
| 1995 | 1,705,263  | 7       | 23,521  |
| 1996 | 2,250,877  | 7       | 27,789  |
| 1997 | 2,580,325  | 5       | 31,856  |
| 1998 | 2,955,193  | 3       | 36,484  |
| 1999 | 3,292,736  | 3       | 40,651  |
| 2000 | 3,055,435  | 3       | 36,484  |
| 2001 | 3,264,907  | 2       | 40,558  |
| 2002 | 3,465,807  | 2       | 43,054  |
| 2003 | 3,465,600  | 1       | 42,523  |
| 2004 | 3,775,292  | 1       | 46,609  |
| 2005 | 4,090,696* | 1       | 50,502  |
| 2006 | 4,248,067* | 1       | 52,445  |
| 2007 | 4,271,867* | 1       | 52,739  |

*Broke AL record.

generate much income, such as the Minnesota Twins (who, incidentally, won 96 games in 2006).

The new Yankee Stadium, scheduled to open in 2009, will seat only about 51,800 fans, making it literally impossible for the team to match its record-setting attendance figure of 2007 (52,739 per game). However, Steinbrenner expects a sharp increase in revenue, due to the new park's luxury suites and shopping venues—as well as increased ticket prices.

Turning a deaf ear to the inevitable protests of Caracciolo and other cash-strapped Yankees fans, Steinbrenner believes he will pack the new house each and every game. Expect four million fans to attend in 2009—and each season ever after.

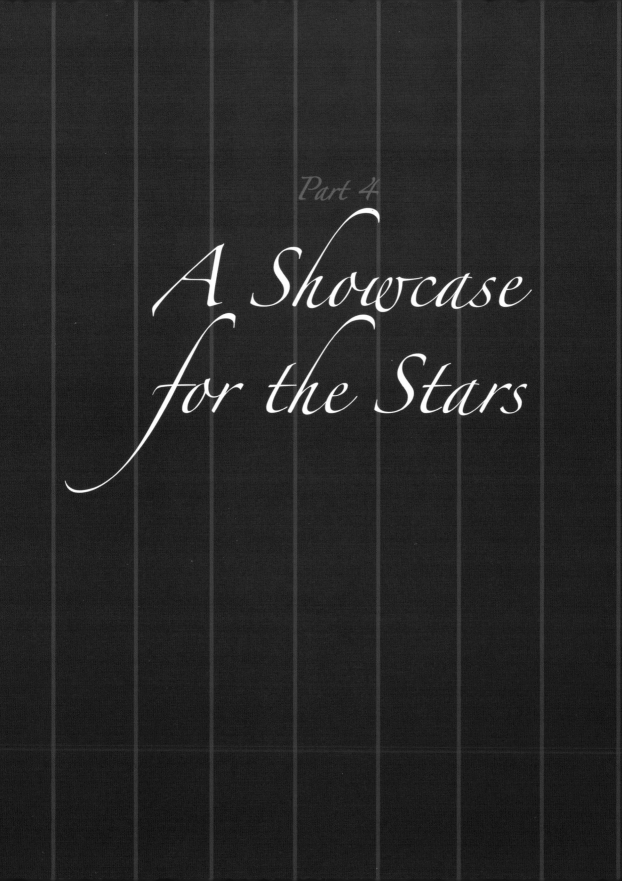

*Part 4*

# A Showcase
# for the Stars

# A Doomed Gehrig Bids Farewell

## July 4, 1939

Gehrig sits out his first game in 15 years on May 2, 1939. Lou realized that his team was better off without him after they beat Detroit 22-2 that day.

**Opposite Page:** Gehrig displayed remarkable strength and courage in his "Luckiest Man" speech, but the overwhelming applause brought even the "Iron Horse" to tears.

Injuries are an expected part of baseball. Tragic illnesses aren't—especially for a player nicknamed the Iron Horse, after an indestructible locomotive. A player hailed by a teammate as "one of the strongest fellows that ever lived." One who played the game with astonishing consistency and brilliance.

Lou Gehrig was a hometown kid from New York who became a Yankee immortal—and the embodiment of the American Dream. The strapping son of German immigrants, he starred in baseball and football at Columbia University in the early 1920s.

Quiet and humble, Gehrig debuted with the Yankees on June 15, 1923. He appeared in 23 games from 1923 to 1924. He appeared as a pinch hitter on June 1, 1925. A day later he was playing first base, when Wally Pipp complained of a headache. So began the legend of the greatest first baseman in baseball history.

Gehrig was a tireless worker, a consummate team man, playing 2,130 consecutive games stretched over 15 seasons. He played through numerous injuries, including a broken thumb, a broken toe, back spasms, and a concussion. Late in his career, doctors spotted 17 different fractures in his hands that had "healed" while he continued to play.

More phenomenal than his dependability was his ability. He amassed a .340 career average (he batted .361 in 34 World Series games) and hit 493 home runs, including a record 23 grand slams. Seven times he drove in more than 150 runs.

Teaming up with Babe Ruth, he was half of the most potent 1-2 punch in the game's history. The low-key Gehrig was always overshadowed by the bombastic Ruth, whom he followed in both the batting order and the fanfare department.

But like Ruth, he would transcend his sport. Though only 36 years old, his sudden health problems became evident early in the 1939 season. He was hitting .143 and struggling with his coordination. He knew it was time to quit "for the good of the team," after he made a routine play in a game against Washington on April 30 and was complimented by pitcher Johnny Murphy. According to *The Sporting News*, Gehrig wondered to himself, "Has it reached that stage?"

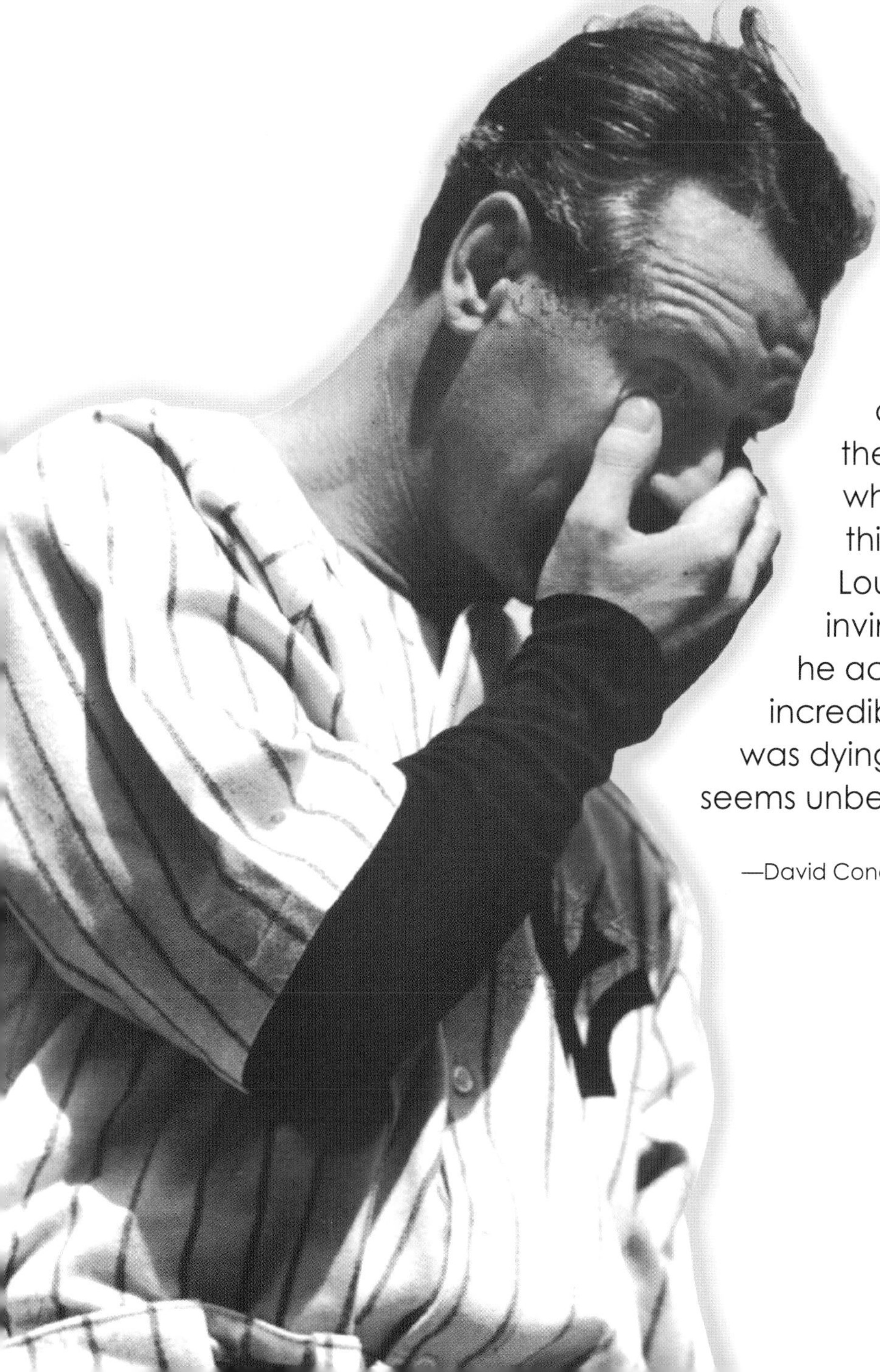

"He
was such
an inspiration,
the courage with
which he faced
this terrible disease.
Lou Gehrig seemed
invincible, and what
he accomplished was
incredible. Knowing he
was dying, his speech still
seems unbelievable."

—David Cone

127

After exhaustive tests, it was found he was suffering from amyotrophic lateral sclerosis—ALS in medical shorthand. Little was then known about the rare degenerative disease, so it was generally believed Gehrig had some form of disability, not necessarily life-threatening. But Gehrig's once-imposing physique was deteriorating.

On July 4, upon the suggestion of writer Paul Gallico (who later wrote the screenplay for the 1942 Gehrig biopic *Pride of the Yankees*, starring Gary Cooper), the Yankees held Lou Gehrig Appreciation Day. Some 61,808 fans packed the stadium, with former teammates, opponents, and dignitaries like Mayor Fiorello LaGuardia lining the field. Gehrig, who had almost collapsed on his arrival at the stadium, was overcome by the thunderous ovation and chants from the crowd. His teammates presented him a trophy with a poem by John Kiernan of *The New York Times* describing him as "Idol of cheering millions."

At first too moved to speak, Gehrig composed himself. In what his biographer Ray Robinson called "baseball's Gettysburg Address," Gehrig, surely knowing his days were coming to an end, delivered his unforgettable farewell speech.

He was a study in dignity, speaking from the heart about being "the luckiest man." His humility and grace that day at Yankee Stadium would touch future generations.

"I was on an American Legion team, and they took us all to see the movie *Pride of the Yankees*. We were in Charlotte, North Carolina, and right then and there I decided I wanted to play for the Yankees. There was so much class associated with the team and Yankee Stadium."

—Bobby Richardson

# The Luckiest Man

Lou Gehrig would die less than two years after delivering his stirring farewell address. But his words on July 4, 1939, delivered in a ceremony between games of a doubleheader against the Washington Senators, remain as vibrant as ever.

*Fans, for the past two weeks you have been reading about a bad break I got. Yet today I consider myself the luckiest man on the face of the earth. I have been in ballparks for 17 years and I have never received anything but kindness and encouragement from you fans.*

*Look at these grand men. Which of you wouldn't consider it the highlight of his career just to associate with them for even one day? Sure I'm lucky. Who wouldn't consider it an honor to have known Jacob Ruppert? Also the builder of baseball's greatest empire, Ed Barrow? To have spent six years with that wonderful little fellow, Miller Huggins? Then to have spent the next nine years with that outstanding leader, that smart student of psychology, the best manager in baseball today, Joe McCarthy? Sure, I'm lucky.*

*When the New York Giants, a team you would give your right arm to beat and vice versa, sends you a gift, that's something. When everybody down to the groundskeepers and those boys in white coats remember you with trophies, that's something. When you have a father and mother who work all their lives so that you can have an education and build your body, it's a blessing. When you have a wife who has been a tower of strength and shown more courage than you dreamed existed, that's the finest I know. So I close in saying that I might have had a bad break, but I have an awful lot to live for.*

# New York's All-Star Cast

## July 11, 1939

Lefty Gomez (left) and Lou Gehrig discuss the quirks of Yankee Stadium with Red Sox slugger Jimmie Foxx. Gehrig was named to the All-Star Game but did not play; he had retired days earlier.

**Opposite Page:** Yankee Stadium is adorned in bunting for the 1939 All-Star Game, the first held at the Stadium. It was pretty much like a Yankees game, as six Bombers started and five went the distance.

By the end of the 1930s, after enduring both the Great Depression and the Dust Bowl, Americans were eager to lose themselves in such popular diversions as movies, big band music, and the national pastime, baseball. The latter was enjoying a long-overdue renaissance, after a decade marred by team-destroying sales and plummeting attendance.

By the late 1930s, however, there were encouraging signs that happy days were indeed here again in Major League Baseball, thanks to such exciting new stars as Joe DiMaggio, Ted Williams, and Bob Feller. Yankee Stadium introduced night baseball. Radio broadcasts proliferated. And in 1939—as part of baseball's centennial celebration—the game's heroes and history were embraced with the dedication of the Baseball Hall of Fame in Cooperstown.

Speaking of heroes, there was also a degree of dominance by the New York Yankees unlike any other major-league team. Starting in 1936, the Yankees would win the world championship four straight years.

Yet the team's biggest star, Lou Gehrig, the powerful Iron Horse, fell mysteriously ill before the '39 season. After playing 2,130 consecutive games, he announced his retirement in June of that year. A month later, Gehrig gave his famous "luckiest man on the face of the earth" speech at Yankee Stadium.

Exactly one week later, on July 11, the stadium was the stage for more memorable theater, the All-Star Game. Created seven years earlier as another novelty to keep fan interest, the 1939 midseason classic came to New York City as part of the festivities connected to the World's Fair.

Nearly 63,000 fans came to the stadium, and Yankees manager Joe McCarthy gave most of them what they wanted. He installed six Yankees, including pitcher Red Ruffing, in the starting lineup, and all his position players went the distance. "Well, you have to play your best men," McCarthy said with a wink. The other starters were Red Rolfe at third, George Selkirk and Joe DiMaggio in the outfield, Joe Gordon at second, and Bill Dickey at catcher.

At least one National League rooter wasn't so thrilled by the pinstriped party. "Make McCarthy play an All-Star American team," he yelled from his box seats. "We can beat them, but we can't beat the Yankees." How right he was. DiMaggio hit a homer in the fifth to give the Yankees—er, the American League—a two-run lead. But the junior circuit was given a major boost by Cleveland's 20-year-old fireballer Bob Feller, who came in relief of Detroit's Tommy Bridges with the bases loaded and one out in the sixth.

Feller had to face Pittsburgh's Arky Vaughan, one of baseball's premier hitters (and nonpareil fastball hitter) in the 1930s. Recounting that moment in his book, *Bob Feller's Little Black Book of Baseball Wisdom*, Feller writes, "Bill Dickey visited the pitcher's mound and conferred with me concerning how to pitch to Vaughan. We decided to throw him a big overhand fastball because we felt that with all of the white shirts in the Yankee Stadium bleachers, the pitch might be disguised a bit and give Vaughan some trouble as to location and speed.

"I threw that ball thinking he might not be able to get around on it, but he did. He hit a hard ground ball to Joe Gordon at second base. Gordon threw to Joe Cronin at shortstop, who in turn covered the bag and then threw to Hank Greenberg at first to end the inning. I pitched the seventh, eighth, and ninth innings, striking out the last two hitters, Johnny Mize and Stan Hack. The American League won the game, 3-1. I was not the winning pitcher, but that was my best All-Star appearance. If

Cleveland phenom Bob Feller, just 20 years old, mowed down the NL All-Star hitters, allowing no runs and just one hit in 3 2/3 innings of relief.

**Opposite Page:** Rookie Ted Williams (left) didn't make the 1939 All-Star Game, but he should have, as he drove in 145 runs, a rookie record, during the season. Joe DiMaggio, the 1939 AL MVP, homered in the midsummer classic.

## A Splendid Debut

Two rainouts and another dreary day cut down attendance at Yankee Stadium for the 1939 season opener between the Yankees and Red Sox. But the 30,278 paying customers were nevertheless very glad they came.

They bore witness to the major-league debut of Boston's ballyhooed 20-year-old rookie, Ted Williams. So much had been heard about the tall, gangly kid, known as The Kid or the Splendid Splinter. Whatever he was called, he was singularly gifted and knew it.

Prior to the opener, a curious United Press reporter asked Williams whom he hit like. "I hit like Ted Williams," he replied.

Williams had earlier told sportswriters, "All I want out of life is that when I walk down the street folks will say, 'There goes the greatest hitter who ever lived.'"

Williams got the attention of folks on his very first day, with a booming double off Red Ruffing that hit the stadium's wall near the 407-foot sign in right-center field. It was Williams' only hit, as Ruffing blanked the Red Sox, 2-0. It was also the only time Williams appeared in a game with Lou Gehrig, who was no longer playing when their teams met again in May.

But the 1939 opener was also notable, since it launched the historic Williams-DiMaggio rivalry. Williams' debut season—.327 with 31 homers and a league-leading 145 RBI—helped spark debate as to whom was the better player: DiMaggio or Williams? Nearly 70 years later, the debate still rages among diehard baseball fans.

there had been such a thing as a save back then, I would have got the credit for one."

Looking back, the 1939 All-Star Game was a highlight event in a season of highlights, especially at Yankee Stadium. The Bronx Bombers were the greatest show in sport. Led by the 24-year-old DiMaggio, who won MVP honors by hitting .381 with 30 homers, the Yankees breezed to an incredible 106-45 record (17 games ahead of the second-place Red Sox).

They became the first All-Star—er, American League—team to win four consecutive pennants. When they swept the Cincinnati Reds in the World Series, it was their record fourth world championship in a row, and eighth in 17 years.

# Babe Ruth Day

## April 27, 1947

Three months after Babe Ruth Day, the Bambino appeared at an American Legion junior all-star game at Philadelphia's Shibe Park. Here he signs a ball for 10-year-old Monica Meehan.

**Opposite Page:** Though barely able to speak, Ruth thanked Yankees fans for their support and gave words of wisdom to aspiring young ballplayers: "If you try hard enough, you're bound to come out on top."

For most Americans, the end of World War II brought fresh hope and a feeling of rebirth. Babe Ruth knew little of it. From 1946 on, he suffered from rejection, depression, intense pain, and the knowledge that he wasn't long for this world.

For Ruth, the first blow came in the form of a letter from Yankees executive Larry MacPhail in 1946. Ruth had asked MacPhail if he could manage the Yankees—his ambition for the previous decade. The Babe said he would even accept the skipper position with Newark, a Yankees farm club. MacPhail responded with a letter to Ruth's home, but when the Babe opened the envelope he read only bad news. Both positions, MacPhail wrote, had been filled. "Babe walked into the kitchen, numb," his wife, Claire, later wrote. "It was the same kitchen where he had sat before on a chair, head in hands, and wept in fury and frustration. He wept once again."

The consensus in baseball was that if Ruth couldn't manage his own life, how could he manage a whole team? Meanwhile, the Babe's health was going the way of his dreams. By 1946, the years of beer, hot dogs, and cigars had taken their toll on the Bambino, who looked older than his age of 51. By that fall, he became concerned about a pain above his left eye. It progressively worsened, and by November the left side of his face was swollen and he couldn't eat solid foods.

Ruth spent a month in the hospital before doctors could diagnose the cause of his illness. The news was the worst imaginable. A malignant tumor, they determined, had grown in the left side of his neck. Babe had surgery on January 5, 1947, but doctors could not remove all the cancer. He remained in the hospital for another month, battling pain and depression. He lost about 100 pounds, and his hair began to fall out. He thought he was going to die.

At the time, Ruth still was the most popular athlete in the country. Thousands of Americans wrote get-well cards and letters to their longtime hero. A seventh-grader from New Jersey sent him a religious medal and words of inspiration: "I know this will be your 61 homer. You will hit it." Babe pinned the medal to his pajamas.

On February 15, Ruth finally left the hospital. Through tears, he acknowledged

the hundreds of well-wishers who saw him emerge from the hospital doors. By Opening Day, Ruth was still in considerable pain. Baseball commissioner Happy Chandler, fearing that the Babe's days were numbered, decided to honor the home run king in grand fashion. He declared that Sunday, April 27, 1947, would be "Babe Ruth Day"—not just at Yankee Stadium, but throughout the major leagues.

Many Yankees fans made sure to attend early church services that day, for they dared not miss the pregame ceremonies. More than 58,000 fans packed the stadium, and those at other ballparks listened to the broadcast on loudspeakers. The event was even broadcast in Latin

America and Japan, where they honored Babu Rusu.

Fans who remembered a hearty Bambino in Yankee pinstripes hardly recognized Ruth when he took the field. Though his camel's-hair overcoat covered his thin frame, his gaunt face and gray hair were visible to all.

The on-field ceremony included an invocation by Francis Cardinal Spellman, the archbishop of New York. Commissioner Chandler, American League President Will Harridge, and National League President Ford Frick all delivered speeches honoring baseball's greatest ambassador. From the American League, Ruth received a bronze plaque in his likeness. The National League offered a leather-bound book with signatures from every NL player. Some players in attendance, including Joe DiMaggio, asked the Babe for his autograph.

Ruth had signed on as a consultant for American Legion baseball. Thus, after the league executives spoke, 13-year-old Larry Cutler expressed his enthusiasm for the Babe's involvement in the youth baseball organization. Then it was Ruth's turn to speak. Yankees announcer Mel Allen introduced the living legend: "And now, ladies and gentlemen, the Bambino, the Sultan of Swat, Babe Ruth!"

In the House That Ruth Built, robust applause cascaded down to the field. Ruth walked up to the cluster of microphones. When the ovation finally subsided, he spoke in a low, raspy voice.

"Thank you very much, ladies and gentlemen," he opened. "You know how bad my voice sounds. Well it feels just as bad. You know this baseball game of ours comes up from the youth. That means the boys. And after you've been a boy, and grow up to know how to play ball, then you come to the boys you see representing themselves today in our national pastime."

Despite his condition, Ruth spoke with enthusiasm and punctuated his words with a clenched fist. He continued: "The only real game in the world, I think, is baseball. As a rule, some people think if you give them a football or a baseball or something like that, naturally, they're athletes right away. But you can't do that in baseball. You've got to start from way down at the bottom, when you're six or seven years old. You can't wait until you're 15 or 16. You've got to let it grow up with you, and if you're successful and you try hard enough, you're bound to come out on top, just like these boys have came to the top now."

Ruth chats with youngsters before leaving for the Babe Ruth Day ceremonies. The day turned out to be exhausting for the ailing legend, who had to leave before the game ended.

**Opposite Page:** Ruth greets New York Giants legend Mel Ott in 1947. At the time, they were the home run kings of their respective leagues. Ott had belted 511 longballs in the NL.

Ruth paused, then concluded: "There's been so many lovely things said about me. I'm glad I had the opportunity to thank everybody. Thank you." Ruth smiled and tipped his cap, and the ceremony ended amid a rain of cheers.

Babe stayed to watch the game, but his wife remembered him feeling awful throughout the afternoon. Through seven innings, the Yankees could not score against the Washington Senators. There was no Ruthian blast, no Five O'Clock Lightning. After DiMaggio grounded out to end the seventh, the Babe decided he needed to leave. The Yankees lost, 1-0.

# The King

Although many of his records have since been broken, Babe Ruth was still baseball's statistical king in 1947. Below are Major League Baseball's stat leaders through 1947, beginning with 1901 (the initial year of the American League).

### Home Runs
| | | |
|---|---|---|
| 1) Babe Ruth | 60 | 1927 |
| 2) Babe Ruth | 59 | 1921 |
| 3) Jimmie Foxx | 58 | 1932 |
| Hank Greenberg | 58 | 1938 |

Career: Ruth 714

### At-bats per Home Run
| | | |
|---|---|---|
| 1) Babe Ruth | 8.46 | 1920 |
| 2) Babe Ruth | 9.00 | 1927 |
| 3) Babe Ruth | 9.15 | 1921 |

Career: Ruth 11.76

### Runs
| | | |
|---|---|---|
| 1) Babe Ruth | 177 | 1921 |
| 2) Lou Gehrig | 167 | 1936 |
| 3) Lou Gehrig | 163 | 1931 |
| Babe Ruth | 163 | 1928 |

Career: Ruth 2,174

### Total Bases
| | | |
|---|---|---|
| 1) Babe Ruth | 457 | 1921 |
| 2) Rogers Hornsby | 450 | 1922 |
| 3) Lou Gehrig | 447 | 1927 |

Career: Ty Cobb 5,854 (61 more than No. 2 Ruth)

### Slugging Percentage
| | | |
|---|---|---|
| 1) Babe Ruth | .849 | 1920 |
| 2) Babe Ruth | .846 | 1921 |
| 3) Babe Ruth | .772 | 1927 |

Career: Ruth .690

### Walks
| | | |
|---|---|---|
| 1) Babe Ruth | 170 | 1923 |
| 2) Ted Williams | 162 | 1947 |
| 3) Ted Williams | 156 | 1946 |

Career: Ruth 2,062

# So Long, Babe

## August 17-18, 1948

At his wake, thousands of children saw Babe Ruth up close for the first and last time. Many wore their baseball uniforms.

**Opposite Page:** On August 17 and 18, upwards of 100,000 people paid their respects at Yankee Stadium. Not since the death of President Roosevelt had America seen such an outpouring of love.

"I honestly don't know anybody who wants to live more than I do." Or so Babe Ruth states at the end of his autobiography, *The Babe Ruth Story*, which he had "told to" writer/ editor Bob Considine. Ruth embraced life, to be sure, on and off the diamond. Even his death, on August 16, 1948, served as an indication of how colossal this slugger was, particularly at Yankee Stadium.

Three weeks before he died of throat cancer, and five days after receiving the last rites of the Roman Catholic Church, Ruth started feeling better. He left Memorial Hospital in Manhattan to attend the film premiere of *The Babe Ruth Story* on July 26, 1948. He had a difficult time during the movie, however, and returned to the hospital on East 68th Street before it was finished. "My obligations are over," Ruth told friends and family from his hospital bed. "I'm going to rest now. I'm going to take it easy."

Tragically, Ruth's condition deteriorated over the next three weeks. Yankee Stadium's greatest legend died at 8:01 P.M. on August 16, 1948, at the age of 53. As word quickly reached his adoring fans, many struggled for words. If there was any consolation, albeit small, it was the fact that Ruth's body would rest in state at Yankee Stadium during the next two days, August 17 and 18, so fans could pay their last respects to him. The heavy-hearted Yankees, their flags lowered to half-staff, had just finished a home stand and were beginning a six-game road trip at the time.

"Newspaper switchboards lit up within minutes after the radio bulletin [confirming Ruth's passing], and were jammed for hours," *Time* magazine reported in its August 30, 1948, edition. "At Memorial Hospital five extra operators were put on, to repeat over and over that Ruth had died."

The House That Ruth Built became a house of tears over the next two days. There are varying reports about how many fans came to bid Ruth a final farewell, as his casket became a centerpiece at the main stadium entrance. Several claim the number exceeded 100,000, the equivalent of two Yankee Stadium sellouts. Others reported a 77,000 total, and still others a figure slightly more or less. This much is certain: Yankee Stadium was supposed to stay

"I was playing for the Newark Bears the same year the Babe died. In 1950, when we won the World Series against Philadelphia, they gave me the Babe Ruth Memorial Award for outstanding performance in the Series. Me being linked somehow to Babe Ruth. Can you imagine?

—Jerry Coleman

open until 10 P.M. the first day. Ruth's widow, Claire, however, asked police to extend the hours until midnight, given the vast numbers still waiting. The actual total will never be known, nor does it matter much.

Far more important was the human evidence of how fans related to this larger-than-life slugger, even after his death. Thousands took the day off from work to stand in front of Ruth's body, if just for a moment. Fathers hoisted their sons and daughters onto their shoulders to catch just a glimpse of the coffin. Some of the children wore their own youth baseball jerseys in honor of Ruth. Hot dog vendors were called to work, selling one of Ruth's favorite foods, even though most of the mourners were too upset to eat. Men, women, boys, and girls wept during two of the most emotional days in Yankee Stadium history.

The following morning, rain clouds opened and put a further damper on the mood. "Even the

"I met the Babe only one time in 1947, the year before he died. Wished like hell I'd asked him for his autograph. I was 16, playing in the Polo Grounds in a high school all-star game, and he shook my hand at home plate. 'How ya doin', Moose?' he said. How can I ever forget it?"

—Moose Skowron

skies wept for The Babe," a taxi driver reportedly said, as he delivered patrons to a funeral mass at St. Patrick's Cathedral. A funeral procession through Manhattan and the Bronx followed the service. Approximately 6,000 mourners jammed the pews for the mass, including pallbearers Joe Dugan and Waite Hoyt, former teammates of Ruth's, who reportedly joked that an adult beverage might be in order. "I'd give a hundred bucks for a cold beer," Dugan reportedly whispered to his friend. "So would the Babe," Hoyt answered, gesturing toward the coffin.

The rain-soaked streets did not prevent thousands more—perhaps as many as 100,000—from bowing their heads and saying farewell, as Ruth's hearse drove 30 miles north to Hawthorne's Gate of Heaven Cemetery in Westchester County. It would be 28 years before his widow joined him in a spot that remains well decorated with tributes to Ruth and the Yankees.

**Opposite Page Left:** The Yankees had just begun a road trip when the Bambino passed away. Here, the players pay a silent tribute to the man who had made the Yankees the greatest team in all of baseball.

**Opposite Page Right:** Men, women, and children file past the casket containing the body of Babe Ruth as it lies in state in the rotunda of Yankee Stadium, on August 18, 1948.

Babe Ruth was pronounced dead at 8:01 P.M. on August 16, 1948. In honor of the beloved legend, the flags at Yankee Stadium were lowered to half-mast.

# New York Press Hails Ruth

In the 1940s, as now, New York's reporters were no strangers to hyperbole. Some journalism from that era, and that city, is considered among the great prose of its time. Other accounts of the news, or what the papers deemed to be the news, probably had discerning readers scratching their heads. Stories about Babe Ruth's 1948 death, and subsequent tributes at Yankee Stadium, fit both categories.

"If he has left a monument behind him, it's the place where he lay in state yesterday, the trace of a thin and seemingly appreciative smile on his tanned face," wrote respected sports columnist Arthur Daley of *The New York Times*. "That place is the Yankee Stadium, the 'House That Ruth Built.'"

Accounts like Daley's left an indelible impression with readers. So much so, in fact, that many fans mistakenly inferred from Daley's tribute that Ruth's body was actually buried in Yankee Stadium as a monument to his greatness. For years, it was one of the Big Apple's most enduring urban myths that Ruth was buried in a center-field monument at the stadium.

Other reporters of the era who penned tributes to the Babe took a far more hard-edged view of the public show of grief surrounding Ruth's death. "No death since Franklin Roosevelt's had moved the people—and the press—to such maudlin excess," stated *Time* magazine in an August 30, 1948, article.

For example, one story described the night scene outside Yankee Stadium, "Urchins from nearby brownstone houses and cold-water flats huddled in the dark ... fighting off tears when the news came." Others quoted the priest from Ruth's mass, deeming his to be "a beautiful death." Some used hokey baseball metaphors about Ruth's final trip "home."

Given Ruth's sense of humor, he probably would have gotten a kick out of it all.

# Saluting the Mick

## June 8, 1969

Mantle's famous No. 7 was retired during the ceremony. All Yankees numbers from 1 to 10 have been retired except Nos. 2 and 6, currently worn by Derek Jeter and Joe Torre, respectively.

**Opposite Page:** June 8, 1969, was proclaimed Mickey Mantle Day in New York City. Here, Mantle receives a plaque from his predecessor in center field, Joe DiMaggio.

The bright sun warmed the afternoon crowd at Yankee Stadium. It was the perfect day for a celebration, and Yankees fans had someone to celebrate. Mickey Mantle had long been a favorite. Any reservations they might have harbored about the strapping Oklahoma teenager, who had taken over center field from Joe DiMaggio in 1952, had been crushed long ago by Mantle's tape-measure home runs, easy speed, and boyish charm.

Drenched in the sun, the Mick didn't appear to have changed much since that April day 18 years earlier, when he'd made his major-league debut with the Yankees. His blue eyes and tanned face still had newspapers and magazines thinking of ways they could justify yet another Mantle cover story. Although his muscular physique today filled out a sharp, navy blue suit, rather than his pinstriped jersey, Mantle's athletic frame was evident—just as it had been when he had first commanded national attention by swatting home runs so far that people were still not certain some had ever landed.

Yes, Mantle's eyes still had that twinkle. On this day, however, they also fought back tears. Mickey Mantle Day at Yankee Stadium, a ceremony to retire his No. 7, had been in the works since Mantle had announced his retirement three months earlier. Several former teammates were among the 61,157 on hand. DiMaggio was there. So was legendary play-by-play man Mel Allen. The Yankees had fired Allen five years earlier, but they knew the impact his soothing Alabama lilt would make in the ceremony, as it had for previous farewell tributes to Ruth, Gehrig, and DiMaggio.

"Ladies and gentlemen, a magnificent Yankee, the great No. 7, Mickey Mantle," Allen proclaimed. On their feet, fans clapped loudly. One minute passed, then two, as Mantle wore an "aw-shucks" look while standing behind the microphones that had been placed at home plate. The applause seemed to get louder. Three minutes elapsed, then four, then five.

Each time Mantle seemed ready to speak, Yankee Stadium's decibel level climbed. Six minutes. Seven minutes. *The New York Times* reported the length of the standing ovation at eight minutes. Other accounts have set the duration at 10 minutes before Yankees president Michael Burke was finally able to silence the crowd for the start of Mantle's speech.

"Just Mickey's presence in the lineup made you feel you were going to win."

—Tom Tresh

Mantle tours the field in a pinstriped cart during his ceremony. The Mick was deeply moved by his adoring fans, especially during their 10-minute ovation before his speech.

Even late in Mantle's career, kids practically broke their necks trying to get his autograph. Balls signed by Mantle during his playing career are worth more than $500 today.

Mantle, who had been uncharacteristically nervous on his way to Yankee Stadium that day, did what he had always done over two decades in the park's home plate area. He came through in the clutch.

"When I walked into the stadium 18 years ago, I guess I felt the same way I feel now," Mantle told the crowd. "I can't describe it. I just want to say that playing 18 years in Yankee Stadium for you folks is the best thing that could ever happen to a ballplayer. Now having my number join 3, 4, and 5 kind of tops everything."

In closing, Mantle alluded to Gehrig's legendary farewell speech, delivered from the same spot 30 years earlier: "I never knew how a man who was going to die could say he was the luckiest man in the world. But now I can understand."

Another thunderous ovation followed the speech. Mantle was then driven around Yankee Stadium in a pinstriped golf cart, adorned with his initials and number on the license plate. Fans screamed as he waved at them, again holding back tears. It was an emotional moment for Mantle, who said he wished everyone in America could experience something like it.

"That's really the moment when I realized it was over," Mantle told biographer Maury Allen several years later, recalling that day in 1969. "I would never play again. I would never be part of the Yankees. I would never hang around the clubhouse, kidding with the other guys. I had to move on. It wasn't easy."

Without Mantle, the Yankees went on to sweep a doubleheader from the Chicago White Sox that day. The scores were 3-1 and 11-2. Moving on, however, was no easier for the Yankee Stadium fans than it was for the Mick.

# Mantle Milestones

Did you know that Mickey Mantle hit more home runs in Yankee Stadium (266) than Babe Ruth (259)? Almost 40 years after hanging up his bat, glove, and spikes, The Mick still owns several Yankee records. Following is a list of club and Yankee Stadium marks held by Mantle to date, i.e., the start of the 2007 season.

### Career

Most games: 2,401
Most at-bats: 8,102
Most Yankee Stadium home runs: 266
Most hits by a switch-hitter: 2,415
Most home runs by a switch-hitter: 536
Most RBI by a switch-hitter: 1,509
Most runs by a switch-hitter: 1,677

### Season

Highest average by a switch-hitter: .365 (1957)
Most home runs by a switch-hitter: 54 (1961)
Most Yankee Stadium home runs by a switch-hitter: 27 (1956)
Most RBI by a switch-hitter: 130 (1956)
Most walks by a switch-hitter: 146 (1957)
Fewest grounded into DP: 2 (1953, 1961), tied with Mickey Rivers (1977)

### Game

Most Yankee Stadium home runs: 3 (5/13/55 vs. Detroit), tied with several players.

| Home run | Date | Place | Pitcher, Team |
|----------|------|-------|---------------|
| No. 1 | May 1, 1951 | Chicago | Randy Gumpert, White Sox |
| No. 100 | June 9, 1955 | New York | Sandy Consuegra, White Sox |
| No. 136* | May 18, 1956 | Chicago | Dixie Howell, White Sox |
| No. 200 | July 26, 1956 | New York | Jim Bunning, Tigers |
| No. 300 | July 4, 1960 | Washington | Hal Woodeshick, Senators |
| No. 400 | Sept. 10, 1962 | Detroit | Hank Aguirre, Tigers |
| No. 500 | May 14, 1967 | New York | Stu Miller, Orioles |
| No. 536** | Sept. 20, 1968 | New York | Jim Lonborg, Red Sox |

\* Passed Ripper Collins to become the all-time home run leader among switch-hitters
\*\* Final big-league home run

"Once you leave and you are not playing anymore, you realize how special it was to be playing here. Just the faces that you see, to me it was Yogi and Mickey and Whitey, the guys you see in spring training. All the guys I played with, Willie Randolph, Ron Guidry. The quality of the people you deal with is amazing. It's been like that over time."

—Don Mattingly

# An All-Star Game at the Bronx Zoo

## July 19, 1977

The relationship between Yankees manager Billy Martin (right) and Reggie Jackson (left) was already a soap opera during the summer of 1977. The All-Star Game brought even more controversy.

A glittering roster of baseball and New York City luminaries was on hand in January 2007, when it was announced that Yankee Stadium would host the 2008 All-Star Game. "When you think of Yankee Stadium," Major League Baseball Commissioner Bud Selig said, "it is, in my opinion, the most famous cathedral in all of sports."

At the time of the announcement, Yankee Stadium had not hosted an All-Star Game in nearly 30 years. And while New Yorkers were looking forward to seeing the 2008 midsummer classic played in the Big Apple, many conceded that the 2008 All-Star Game couldn't possibly eclipse the memory of the dramatic 1977 game.

The 1977 season had been the proverbial mixed bag for the Yankees and their colorful manager, Billy Martin. On the positive side, they were squarely back on top as a big-league power. They had followed their 1976 pennant with 100 regular-season wins and their first World Series championship since '62. How could any of their fans be unhappy with that?

There were some major bumps in the road, however. Before the season began, a comment by their star slugger, Reggie Jackson, describing himself as "the straw that stirs the drink," had not sat well with some of his teammates. A controversial incident at Fenway Park on June 18 saw Martin pull Jackson from a game for not hustling in the outfield; a national television audience watched the ensuing eruption between manager and player, who had to be physically restrained from one another in the dugout.

One month and a day after that blowup, the newly renovated Yankee Stadium rolled out the red carpet for an All-Star Game for the first time since 1960. A sellout crowd of 56,683 was in attendance on July 19, 1977. So was Martin, as skipper of the American League squad, and Jackson as its right fielder. Conspicuously absent, however, was dominant pitcher Nolan Ryan of the California Angels. Despite his 13 victories and incredible 234 strikeouts at the All-Star break, the flame-throwing ace had been left off Martin's roster, under a format that held that each team had to be represented by at least one player. Just a month before the All-Star Game, Ryan had struck out 19 men in a game, exacerbating the level of the "snub." Noted Jim Palmer, the AL's starter, "It's a bad system."

Philadelphia's Mike Schmidt barrels into second base
as Yankees second sacker Willie Randolph attempts
to turn a double play. Randolph, who went 1-for-5,
was the only player on either team to play the entire
game.

Fate then seemingly intervened, but to no avail. Both Frank Tanana of the Angels and Mark Fidrych of the Tigers had arm injuries and were unable to pitch. So the day before the game, Martin called Ryan and asked if he would fly to New York as a late roster addition. Ryan flatly refused.

True to form, Martin went ballistic and launched into one of his notorious tirades, declaring that "Ryan should be suspended and not receive his salary for a week. I think baseball should dictate policy to the players and not let the players dictate policy to baseball." In a final swipe at Ryan, Martin vowed he'd never include him on any All-Star club he managed.

Ryan, a fierce competitor, was not thrilled to have been left off the initial roster, but later said it had nothing to do with his decline of Martin's last-minute offer. He had already made plans with his family over the three-day break, and did not want to travel from California to New York on one day's notice. "I also had been on the team before," he noted in his autobiography, *Throwing Heat*, "and thought it was a good opportunity for them to give some other deserving pitcher a chance."

It turned out the American League could have used Ryan's help. Before the game, National League manager Sparky Anderson told reporters, "The only reason we're here is to kick the living hell out of those guys," turning up the heat on a game that does not count in the standings. Joe Morgan led off with a home run off Palmer, and the NL was well on its way. Greg Luzinski added a two-run shot later in his club's four-run first inning, and after three frames, the NL held a 5-0 cushion.

Martin and the American League made a game of it. In the end, however, Yankee Stadium's million-dollar scoreboard read National League 7, American League 5. Martin's first All-Star Game defeat was, in many ways, a painful one.

"Everything about 1977 had some kind of controversy. I remember Billy [Martin] was managing us [the American League] and being pretty upset that Nolan Ryan declined to participate. Jim Palmer started and got hit pretty hard. When Billy went to take him out, Palmer said, 'What took you so long? I thought you wanted to win this game.'"

—Graig Nettles

**Opposite Page:** Nolan Ryan had 234 strikeouts at the All-Star break but wasn't initially selected for the game. When Billy Martin invited him at the last minute, Ryan said no thanks.

# 1960 All-Star Game

Though Yankee Stadium hosted more championship baseball games than any major league venue in the 20th century, only three All-Star Games were contested there prior to the scheduled 2008 game. The '77 and '39 editions are featured in this chapter. Yankee Stadium's "other" midsummer classic, staged in 1960, was not a classic but featured some milestones.

It was played during the era when two All-Star Games were the norm. Two days earlier, in Kansas City, the National League jumped to a 5-0 lead in the first three innings, and held on for a 5-3 win in 100-degree heat. When the stars reconvened in the Bronx on July 13, temperatures were lower and the reception was downright cool—less than 39,000 fans turned out at Yankee Stadium. Those who were on hand saw a one-sided affair. Vern Law, who saved the first game for the NL, started and earned a 6-0 victory in this one. Eddie Mathews hit a two-run home run in the second inning off Whitey Ford that turned out to be all the offense his side needed. Willie Mays, Stan Musial, and Ken Boyer also homered. Musial's blast, a towering drive into the third-tier, right-field stands, was his sixth All-Star Game home run, establishing an All-Star Game career record.

One of the biggest draws for Yankee Stadium patrons was the return of Mays to the Big Apple. His Giants had moved from New York to San Francisco after the 1957 season. It also marked the 18th and final All-Star Game for Boston's Ted Williams.

# Farewell, Captain

## September 20, 1980

Thurman Munson had taken pilot lessons so that he could fly home to his family on off-days.

**Opposite Page:** Accompanied by Bobby Murcer, Thurman Munson's widow, Diana, reads a plaque dedicated to her late husband during the 1980 ceremony. Munson's No. 15 was retired on that day.

In Yankee Stadium history, August 2, 1979, remains the most sorrowful day, an unfathomable loss. The tragic death of Thurman Munson, the 32-year-old captain and spirit of three consecutive pennant-winning teams, still seems surreal. A man in the prime of his career. A family man. A leader. The shocking news of Munson's fatal plane crash left an embedded memory in Yankee Stadium, where his clubhouse locker remains vacant. And it lives in Monument Park, where the Yankees erected a plaque for him.

Gruff and tough, Thurman Lee Munson was a fierce competitor who won the admiration of foes and teammates alike with his hustle, determination, and pride. The son of a long-haul truck driver, Munson became a blue-collar hero for leading the Yankees to back-to-back world championships in 1977-78.

"When you look at the way he played and the way he carried himself," said teammate Chris Chambliss, "it was the way you wanted to play. That's what made him captain."

The Yankees' captain certainly boasted star credentials. Munson was Rookie of the Year in 1970 and Most Valuable Player in 1976, won three consecutive Gold Gloves, and hit over .300 five times. Yet, he never acted like a star, or looked like one. Some teammates called him Squatty Body, but nobody garnered more respect. The consummate gamer, he did whatever it took to win, and his confidence was infectious.

"He felt he belonged the first time he stepped on the field here at Yankee Stadium," recalled Bobby Murcer, his close friend and teammate.

That was in 1969, when Munson played 26 games. He came up in the middle of a not-so-glorious era for the Yankees. Mickey Mantle had just retired, and the Mets were making magic. Mired in mediocrity, the Yankees teams at that time were perhaps most noted for Horace Clarke, the oft-criticized second baseman from the Virgin Islands. Remember the forgettable Horace Clarke era?

As much as any single player, Munson helped restore pride in the pinstripes. He became the regular catcher and backbone of the team in the 1970s, playing every day, hurt or not. He was a clutch hitter and masterfully handled the pitching staff.

THURMAN MUNSON
NEW YORK YANKEES
NE 7, 1947 - AUGUST 2, 1979
YANKEE CAPTAIN

UR CAPTAIN AND LEADER HAS NOT
FT US-
ODAY, TOMORROW, THIS YEAR, NEXT...
UR ENDEAVORS WILL REFLECT OUR
OVE AND ADMIRATION FOR HIM."

ERECTED BY
THE NEW YORK YANKEES

"When I came back here to the Yankees, Thurman and I started having these long talks. We talked about what we were going to do now that we were getting to the part of … well, the second part of our lives. Thurm was the kind of guy who could have sat back and really appreciated his family and what he had done in his career. But he never got the chance."

—Bobby Murcer

So respected was Munson that in 1976, manager Billy Martin called him aside and told him owner George Steinbrenner wanted the team "to have sort of an official team leader … and we agreed that you're the best choice for the job."

Munson became the team's first captain since Lou Gehrig. It was an honor not even bestowed on DiMaggio or Mantle. Munson was indeed Mr. Yankee, and not even Reggie Jackson's loud arrival in 1977—and indirect swipe at Munson with his notorious "I'm the straw that stirs the drink" comment—changed Munson's esteemed stature in the clubhouse.

Munson's devotion to his family never changed either. He owned a private plane, and flew home to Canton, Ohio, to be with them as much as he could. Trying to land his twin-engine jet on a trip during an off day, the plane caught fire, killing him.

The entire Yankees team attended the funeral in Canton, Ohio, where Murcer and Lou Piniella gave moving eulogies. Later that same day, in as heart-wrenching a game ever played at the stadium, Murcer drove in all five runs as the Yankees beat Baltimore, 5-4, and gave Diana Munson the bat he used to honor her husband.

"I hate to say this, but I don't know if today's players truly realize what a great player Thurman was, what a great captain, a great leader. In my last year [1975] he was just turning the corner to become that. His empty locker in the clubhouse is a sad and powerful reminder. When players see it, they know he was special but they don't really know."

—Mel Stottlemyre

Just over a year later, prior to a late-season game against the Boston Red Sox, Murcer, Piniella, and Gene Michael presented Diana with her late husband's No. 15, and then unveiled the eighth plaque to be displayed in Monument Park. Many in the crowd of 50,257 had to wipe away tears as the plaque's engraved words, written by George Steinbrenner, flashed on the scoreboard: "Our captain and leader has not left us, today, tomorrow, this year, next…. Our endeavors will reflect our love and admiration for him."

**Opposite Page Left:** While he practiced takeoffs and landings in his hometown of Akron, Ohio, Munson's plane hit a tree and burst into flames. Two companions were injured; Munson likely died from asphyxiation.

**Opposite Page Right:** Yankees third baseman Graig Nettles pays homage to his former captain on August 3, a day after Munson's death. The entire team attended the funeral in Canton, Ohio.

The Yankees bow their heads during a memorial service for Munson on August 5. A day after the funeral, New York beat Baltimore 5-4 as Munson's good friend, Bobby Murcer, drove in all five runs.

# Honoring Elston Howard

Fifteen months after Thurman Munson's death, the Yankees mourned the premature loss of another legendary catcher: Elston Howard.

Howard was the first black Yankee, a classy and respected member of nine pennant-winning teams. When he joined the team in 1955, eight years after Jackie Robinson broke baseball's color barrier, the Yankees were the 13th of 16 teams to include a black player.

The Yankees' tardiness in signing a black player before Howard was criticized by social activists. Some picketed Yankee Stadium in the early 1950s, and Robinson also implored Yankees management to integrate its team.

When 26-year-old Howard joined the team, he had no complaints, saying, "No one in the Yankee organization made me conscious of my color." He would eventually replace Yogi Berra as catcher and became a four-time All-Star. He was the first African American to win the Most Valuable Player award in the American League (1963), and then became the first black coach in the AL, joining the Yankees staff in 1969 after he retired.

A beloved figure as player and coach in Yankee Stadium, Howard followed Bill Dickey and Berra in the lineage of great Yankee's catchers. Then he became a great help to Munson, who continued the tradition.

He was only 51 when he died. Four years later, his No. 32 was retired and a plaque honoring him was placed in Monument Park. It reads: "Elston Howard: A man of great gentleness and dignity."

# A Day for Scooter

## August 4, 1985

Rizzuto clutches his retired jersey during the August 4 ceremony. After Rizzuto's playing days, many Yankees wore No. 10, including Tony Kubek, Dick Howser, and Chris Chambliss.

**Opposite Page:** Even the perpetually downcast Billy Martin offers applause and a smile for Rizzuto, his keystone companion from 1950 to '57.

Holy cow! There was a Phil Rizzuto Day at Yankee Stadium, on August 4, 1985. Several members of the superb Yankees teams of the late 1940s and early 1950s were brought together for the occasion. They gathered about Rizzuto near home plate, listening with approval as the master of ceremonies on the field spoke in glowing terms of their celebrated former teammate.

Rizzuto took over for Frank Crosetti as the Yankees shortstop in 1941 and played his entire career in the Bronx, spanning the years of the Yankees' greatest dynasty. He overcame his diminutive size—generously listed as 5-foot-6, 160 pounds—to anchor Yankees teams that won seven World Series titles, including an unprecedented five in a row, from 1949 to 1953.

Following his retirement in 1956, Rizzuto moved right into the Bombers' broadcasting booth, where he manned the microphone as the voice of the Yankees for another 40 years. Rizzuto spoke a unique language of malapropisms and non sequiturs, and he was a shameless homer announcer. His distinctive cry of "Holy cow!" was the rallying call of Yankees fans for two generations.

As part of the pregame festivities, the Yankees brought on the field a cow wearing a halo. The angelic bovine accidentally stepped on Rizzuto's foot, knocking the elegant 67-year-old honoree to the ground. Holy cow, indeed! Hushed thousands watched and waited for Rizzuto to regain his feet (and his dignity). He did so gracefully, waving to the rows of relieved, smiling faces that walled the stadium. Then the crowd, along with former Yankees greats Joe DiMaggio, Mickey Mantle, Whitey Ford, Hank Bauer, and Tommy Henrich, proudly watched as Rizzuto's No. 10 jersey was retired, and a Monument Park plaque was dedicated to the lifelong Yankee.

Born in Brooklyn, the son of a trolley car conductor, Philip Francis Rizzuto was affectionately known as Scooter. To fans of an earlier time lucky enough to see him glide after a ball in the third-base hole, or flash up the middle to snare a grounder, the moniker was a perfect fit.

"Gosh, Phil was just a great guy, funny with those superstitions. Always wore gum on the button of his cap. What I remember most is when I was a rookie and he took me out to dinner. He said, 'Moose, when you're a veteran and making more money, you better take care of the rookies.' I never forgot that. Team effort, that's what guys like Phil taught me."

—Moose Skowron

Scooter wore the pinstripes for 13 seasons with flair—and a wad of gum on the button of his cap.

He played with a youthful exuberance, but he was dead serious about winning. Unfazed by pressure, Rizzuto performed at his best in October. In fact, he played in 52 World Series games—the most of any shortstop—and made just five errors. He played in 21 consecutive Series games without an error. So reliably did he make the routine play that pitcher Vic Raschi once told a reporter, "My best pitch is anything the batter grounds, lines, or pops up in the direction of Rizzuto."

Stellar defense made Rizzuto a difference maker, but he was also a catalyst at the top of the batting order. He peaked offensively in 1950, reaching career highs with a .324 batting average and 125 runs scored. He won the American League's Most Valuable Player award that year, and the next year he was MVP of the World Series.

Slick fielding and intelligent leadership, however, are assets not easily quantified, so Hall of Fame voters annually underestimated

In his day, Rizzuto brought spirit, speed, defense, and a solid bat to the Yankees' attack. When he batted .324 in 1950, he won the AL MVP award.

Rizzuto receives a set of golf clubs and a farm animal with a halo—a real, live holy cow.

"Phil was my buddy, everyone loved him. Gosh, we had an awful lot of good times together. I know everyone on the Yankees protected him like a little brother. My first spring training [1947] we were in Venezuela and the security guards wouldn't let him in the stadium, not believing he was a ballplayer. We had to tell them he was our shortstop."

—Yogi Berra

Rizzuto's deserving credentials. Throughout the years of being passed over for the Hall of Fame, he had said he would accept entrance any way into Cooperstown: "If they want a batboy, I'll go in as a batboy."

Suddenly, the microphone was thrust at Rizzuto. When he said that having his number retired by the Yankees meant more to him than making the Hall of Fame, the ecstatic crowd erupted into a prolonged ovation. To Rizzuto, it must have felt like a group hug from a loving family.

In 1994, 38 years after his retirement, the Scooter finally did get the call telling him that he'd been voted into the Hall of Fame.

Those huckleberries are still looking for a batboy.

# Seaver Wins 300th

Phil Rizzuto Day was held during a pregame ceremony before the Yankees took on the Chicago White Sox. Most of the crowd of 54,032 filing excitedly into Yankee Stadium on that sunny, Sunday afternoon in the Bronx had come out to honor Rizzuto, the legendary shortstop and loveable broadcaster. But some had come out to witness another New York icon, Tom Seaver, now pitching for Chicago, try for his 300th career victory.

It turned out to be a terrific day.

Returning to the city where he began his great career in 1967, as a 22-year-old Mets phenom, Seaver, now 40, pitched a six-hit, 4-1, complete-game victory. When Don Baylor hit a high fly to left field on Seaver's 145th pitch for the final out, the crowd roared its appreciation for the pitcher who had turned New York's National League team, the Mets, from loveable losers into world champions. Seaver embraced his wife and children near the visitors' dugout, and was presented an engraved bowl from the Yankees' representative, pitcher Phil Niekro, who would win his 300th game in Toronto on the last day of the season.

Emotionally drained but overjoyed, Seaver became only the 17th pitcher in major-league history to reach 300 wins—and the first ever to achieve the feat at Yankee Stadium.

Several years later, when Rizzuto and Seaver were paired as Yankees announcing partners, a common topic of conversation was the irony of that day's scheduling coincidence. While listening to Rizzuto's reminisces, one could sense in his voice a nagging regret. While it is understandable why Yankees fans would want to witness Seaver make history, the game played on Phil Rizzuto Day may have been the only time that Yankees fans ever rooted against their home team at Yankee Stadium.

# A Final Tribute for Joltin' Joe

## September 27, 1998

What do you give an 83-year-old Joe DiMaggio? The one important thing that he lacked: eight World Series rings. His original set had been stolen from his motel room back in 1960.

**Opposite Page:** DiMaggio takes a drive around the field for one last hurrah. For 62 years, the Yankee Clipper had grown accustomed to thunderous applause whenever he stepped on the field.

From the very first day Joe DiMaggio set foot in Yankee Stadium in 1936, to the last game he played in 1951, the Yankee Clipper had been something special. A baseball deity in classic pinstripes with No. 5 on the back. And so they came out to honor DiMaggio at Yankee Stadium, 62 years after his spectacular, major-league debut.

The Yankees had once again regained their exalted status as baseball's elite team. In Joe Torre's third campaign as the Yankees manager, he had one world championship under his belt. The 1998 team entered the final game of the season against the Tampa Bay Devil Rays with 113 wins—a fitting time if ever there was one to pay tribute to DiMaggio, a man who personified the dignity of being a Yankee.

Babe Ruth may have been the most talented player to ever play for the Yankees, but DiMaggio was perhaps the most popular player in the team's history.

A crowd of over 50,000 showed up for the Sunday afternoon affair, lit by a brilliant sun. When DiMaggio first stepped onto the field, the fans stared in awe at the American icon, who had once hit safely in 56 consecutive games and married the ultimate sex symbol, Marilyn Monroe. And even though the calendar had changed DiMaggio's once dark hair to white, he still managed to retain a regal flair at age 83. However, there was an undertow of sadness to the otherwise festive occasion, for many suspected that this public gathering might be the last time the great DiMaggio appeared at Yankee Stadium.

Singer Paul Simon sang from "Mrs. Robinson," highlighted by the passage, "Where have you gone, Joe DiMaggio? Our nation turns its lonely eyes to you. … Joltin' Joe has left and gone away."

New York Mayor Rudolph Giuliani issued a proclamation that honored DiMaggio for his part in establishing the Yankees as the most recognizable sports franchise in the world.

On one hand, DiMaggio wore his 1936 World Series ring, which commemorated one of the nine championship teams he had played on while gracing center field for the Yankees. In 1960, DiMaggio had been wearing the 1936 ring when thieves stole the other eight championship rings from his hotel room in Alaska, where he'd been vacationing.

Yankees owner George Steinbrenner provided the day's happiest surprise for DiMaggio when he had Phil Rizzuto make a presentation to DiMaggio behind home plate. Rizzuto had been DiMaggio's teammate and friend, so it meant more to have the Scooter present him with Steinbrenner's gift: replicas of those eight, diamond-studded World Series rings, arranged neatly in a case. In addition, Steinbrenner awarded DiMaggio replicas of the Yankees' 1977 and 1996 championship rings.

DiMaggio eventually moved to a microphone to make few remarks, but when he spoke, nothing could be heard. He tapped the microphone a couple of times, yet it refused to work, so he did not address the crowd. He instead stepped inside a white 1956 Thunderbird convertible for a lap around the stadium.

"Never got to play with Joe, but he was always nice to me. He used to dress in my locker for Old-Timers' Day, and he took me and Tony Kubek to dinner afterward. Once he even invited us to dinner when he was with Marilyn [Monroe]. Joe was class, all right. He helped make the Yankees what they are."

—Moose Skowron

At the end of the day, the Yankees won their 114th game of the season, Yankees center fielder Bernie Williams became the eighth Yankee to win a batting title—DiMaggio was the only Yankee to win two—and Yankees fans got their final glimpse of Joltin' Joe in Yankee Stadium. DiMaggio died prior to the beginning of the next baseball season.

In 1996, at age 81, DiMaggio tosses out a ceremonial first pitch. Joe made several appearances at Yankee Stadium in his later years.

Joe Girardi, Chuck Knoblauch, Jose Cardenal, and Mariano Rivera watch a tribute to Joltin' Joe on the Yankee scoreboard.

"Right off the bat he was my hero. He was the first player that I noticed as a kid growing up in Astoria. When I got the chance to play with him, I couldn't believe I was on the mound and he was in center field."

—Whitey Ford

# The Man Who Wouldn't Fan

Joe DiMaggio accomplished many feats as a player. The 56-game hitting streak in 1941 is the accomplishment most remembered. Most feel this record will never be broken, due to the sheer difficulty of the task, as well as the increased media scrutiny that would make pursuing DiMaggio's record even more difficult.

While the consecutive games hitting streak is impressive, the Yankee Clipper achieved another accomplishment that flies under the radar of recognition, and it cuts to the heart of why he could put together such a prolonged hitting streak.

DiMaggio was one of the most difficult players to strike out in major-league history—particularly for a hitter with power. Perhaps this can be attributed to the wide stance he employed or his great eye, or it could have been a combination of both. Whatever the reason, DiMaggio's strikeout numbers were just short of amazing for a player who took a cut at the ball like he did.

In 1941, DiMaggio had 541 at-bats and struck out just 13 times. Other seasons saw him strike out 18, 20, 21, and 24 times. When the final ledger for DiMaggio's career was struck, Joltin' Joe had just 369 strikeouts in 6,821 at-bats, which translated to just eight more strikeouts than home runs.

To gain a full appreciation of what DiMaggio accomplished, compare his numbers to those of other noted sluggers—Henry Aaron, who finished with 755 career home runs, had 1,383 strikeouts. Or consider the record of Jose Canseco, who finished with 462 home runs and 1,942 strikeouts. In short, Joe DiMaggio could put the bat on the ball.

# Four for Five for No. 2

## October 26, 2000

Jeter signifies his fourth world championship in five years after celebrating the Yankees' 4-2 win over the Mets in Game 5 of the 2000 World Series.

**Opposite Page:** Jeter (right) high-fives David Justice after the latter's three-run homer in the seventh inning of Game 6 of the 2000 ALCS. New York won 9-7 to clinch the series, even though Seattle had won 29 more games than the Yankees during the season (116 to 87).

On a late New York night in 2000, a male youth—with his cap on backwards and surrounded by cops—stuck four fingers in the air in what looked like a provocative gesture. Instead of handcuffing the "punk," the police probably wanted to hug the handsome fella. After all, this was Derek Jeter, celebrating in the Yankees' clubhouse, and his four fingers signified the number of world championships he had won in his brief career.

Born in Pequannock, New Jersey, Jeter was raised in Kalamazoo, Michigan. The notion that he would grow up to play shortstop (his favorite position) for the Yankees (his favorite team) and win four world titles (by the age of 26) seemed about as far-fetched as George Steinbrenner sticking with the same manager for a dozen years. Yet DJ's dreams came true in rapid-fire succession.

Drafted in the first round (sixth overall) by the Yankees in 1992, Jeter premiered with the Bombers three years later. "I hope I wear this jersey forever," the fresh-faced phenom beamed. While jersey numbers 5 (DiMaggio), 4 (Gehrig), and 3 (Ruth) were retired, Derek wore number 2. Like those immortals, Jeter would lead New York to multiple world titles early in his Yankees career.

By 1996, the Yankees hadn't won a championship in 18 years, but Jeter brought a much-needed spark to the team. Not only could he pick it at shortstop, but he infused the lineup with positive energy, base-stealing speed, and .300-hitting punch. That season's Rookie of the Year, he proceeded to make the 1996 postseason his own personal showcase. He ripped .412 in the ALDS and .417 in the ALCS before scoring five runs in the World Series victory over Atlanta. Said Joe Torre, "The tougher the situation, the more fire he gets in his eyes."

For the rest of the decade, Jeter reigned as baseball's hottest young star. He belted two homers in the 1997 Division Series loss to Cleveland, then smashed .353 in New York's sweep of San Diego in the 1998 World Series. In 1999, Jeter enjoyed one of the greatest seasons ever for a shortstop, ripping .349 with 24 homers, 219 hits, and 134 runs. As New York blazed through the 1999 postseason (going 11-1), Jeter led the way with a .375 average.

Meanwhile, gossip columnists couldn't keep up with Derek's succession of glamorous

From 2004 through 2007, the Yankees boasted, unquestionably, the greatest left side of the infield in baseball history, with Alex Rodriguez (left) at third base and Jeter at shortstop. It was certainly the most expensive duo, with their combined salaries topping $40 million.

Paul Cherubino of West Babylon, New York, proudly displays the uniform of his favorite player. Of Yankee uniform numbers 1 through 10, only 2 (Jeter) and 6 (Joe Torre) have not been retired—but they undoubtedly will be.

girlfriends, beginning with pop diva Mariah Carey. Jeter outdid DiMaggio's marriage to Marilyn Monroe by dating Hollywood starlets, supermodels, a former Miss Universe, and a former Miss Teen USA. And so that envious men could smell just like him, Derek came out with his own cologne: Driven.

In 2007, Jeter reached the playoffs for the 12th consecutive season. He held career MLB postseason records for hits, runs, and total bases. Through it all, October 2000 stands out as the pinnacle of his career. After smashing .339 during the season and winning the All-Star Game MVP award, he smacked .317 in the postseason and came through again and again in clutch situations.

En route to a five-game ALDS triumph over Oakland, Derek drove in two runs in Game 3—a 4-2 Yankees win. Pundits raved about how the top of the order—Jeter, Bernie Williams, Paul O'Neill, and others—was able to manufacture runs. They got on base, moved runners along, and came through with the big hits. Even in the 2000 ALCS against the Mariners, who had won 116 games during the season, New York won in six games, with Jeter delivering key hits, runs, homers, and/or RBI in all the victories.

With the Mets prevailing in the 2000 NLCS, all of New York geared up for the first intracity World Series in 44 years. *Newsweek* featured Jeter and Mets catcher Mike Piazza on its cover. "New York! New York!" the headline proclaimed. "Hooray for the Subway Series."

While the iconic moment of the 2000 fall classic featured Roger Clemens throwing half of a broken bat at Piazza, Jeter was the true star of the Series. In Game 1 at Yankee Stadium, he gunned down Timo Perez at home plate in the sixth to preserve a scoreless game. Jeter reached base three times and scored once as the Yankees won 4-3 in the 12th on Jose Vizcaino's single. In Game 2, his two doubles keyed a 6-5 Bombers victory—their 14th consecutive triumph in World Series action.

After the Mets ended the streak in Game 3, Jeter almost singlehandedly won Game 4, as he homered, tripled, and scored twice in a 3-2 victory. In Game 5 at Shea Stadium, he tied the game at 2-2 with a solo homer in the sixth. Luis Sojo's two-run single in the ninth made it 4-2, and Mariano Rivera slammed the door in the bottom of the frame.

In the locker room, the Yankees chanted "Three-peat! Three-peat" after becoming the first team since the 1972-74 Oakland A's to win three straight world titles. For Jeter, who was named the World Series MVP, it was four titles in five tries. With his four-finger gesture, he made sure everyone knew it.

# Jeter's Shining Moments

- Named AL Rookie of the Year in 1996.
- Won the world championship in 1996 and 1998-2000.
- Played in six World Series.
- Voted MVP of the 2000 World Series.
- Named MVP of the 2000 All-Star Game.
- Won his third straight Gold Glove Award in 2006.
- Has finished in the Top 10 in AL MVP voting six times, including second in 2006.
- Won the 2006 AL Hank Aaron Award (.343-14-97).
- An eight-time All-Star.
- Set still-standing career highs in batting (.349), runs (134), hits (219), homers (24), RBI (102), triples (nine), walks (91), total bases (346), OBP (.438), and SLG (.552) in 1999.
- Has topped 200 hits six times, 30 steals three times, .330 three times, 100 runs 11 times, and 10 homers 12 times.
- Ranks fifth among active players in career average (.317).
- Cracked his 2,000th hit at age 31.
- Led the league in runs (127) in 1998.
- Ranks second in the majors in hits during the 2000s (1,504).
- Holds MLB career postseason records for hits, runs, and total bases.
- Belted the first November home run in baseball history to win Game 4 of the 2001 World Series.
- Named captain of the Yankees in 2003.
- On the Yankees' career lists, ranks first in singles (1,721), second in steals (264), fourth in hits (2,356), fifth in batting (.317) and runs (1,379), and sixth in doubles (386).

# Part 5

# Not Just Baseball

# One for the Gipper

## November 10, 1928

*College Football News* rated Gipp as the fourth greatest college football player of all time. During World War II, the U.S. liberty ship *George Gipp* was named in his honor.

The 85,000 football fans who packed Yankee Stadium tried to kill the time. Sitting through intermission of the annual Notre Dame-Army game, they waited in line for hot dogs, went to the restroom, and huddled against the cold. None of them knew that in the bowels of the stadium, Notre Dame coach Knute Rockne was delivering the most immortal locker room speech in the history of sports.

The first Notre Dame-Army game had been staged at West Point in 1913, but the rivalry became so huge that only Yankee Stadium could contain it. Massive crowds packed the stadium during the Roaring Twenties to witness this ethnic/religious rivalry: America's Catholics versus the old establishment. At halftime in 1928, the game between the 4-2 Fighting Irish and the undefeated, seemingly indomitable Cadets was scoreless.

If Notre Dame was to win this game, Rockne believed, they would need a powerful dose of inspiration. So during halftime, he proceeded to tell his players the story of George Gipp, the quiet, likeable All-American of the post-Great War era. In an epic performance in 1920, Gipp had amassed 480 total yards against Army. He died of pneumonia that very fall, but on his deathbed, he had whispered to Rockne, "Someday, Rock, when things on the field are going against us, tell the boys, Rock, to go out and win just one for the Gipper. I don't know where I'll be then, Coach. But I'll know about it, and I'll be happy."

Rockne's story brought his players to tears, and they burst out of the locker room, ready to crush the Army juggernaut. Trailing 6-0 in the third quarter, Nortre Dame's Jack Chevigny stormed in for a touchdown. "That's one for the Gipper," he said. "Let's get another." Later in the game, the Irish broke the 6-6 tie when gangly receiver Johnny O'Brien scored on a 32-yard touchdown pass, earning a hug from Rockne. Notre Dame pulled off a monumental upset, winning 12-6.

Much of the crowd roared its approval. The Fighting Irish had won a game for ol' Notre Dame, and for America's Catholics. More importantly, they had won one for the Gipper.

# Louis' Nazi Knockout

## June 22, 1938

Joe Louis did not kill Max Schmeling, like he feared he would, but he did beat him senseless. Referee Arthur Donovan ended the fight before the end of the first round.

Two years earlier, after defeating Joe Louis, Max Schmeling had left Yankee Stadium as world heavyweight champion. He later dined with Adolf Hitler and was touted as the Aryan Superman—the man who had proven the superiority of the white race.

Now Schmeling was back in the stadium for a rematch with the Brown Bomber, and this time, he was feeling the pressure. He knew that a loss to a man of a supposedly inferior race would humiliate the Nazi Party and anger Hitler. In fact, he had received a phone call, laden with implications, from the *Führer* earlier in the day.

Although Hitler would not initiate the Second World War until 1939, by June of 1938, his regime was already known for its brutality. The Nazis crushed civil liberties within Germany, persecuted Jews, and occupied Austria; they were also building a military intended for continental domination. Some New Yorkers empathized with Nazi ideology, but freedom lovers in general—and Jews and African Americans in particular—despised Nazism. Though not a Nazi himself, Schmeling was the regime's poster boy.

As Schmeling made his way to the ring, the wrath of those in attendance descended upon him. According to his autobiography, fans spat at him and pelted him with soda cups, banana peels, and packs of cigarettes. "Not excitement or curiosity awaited me, but sheer hatred," he wrote. "Never in my life did 100 meters seem this long. I could not defend myself against the feeling that I was going to the guillotine."

When he climbed into the ring, Schmeling faced the man who was ready to chop his head off. Louis sought revenge for the one loss of his career, a shocking 12-round knockout by Schmeling in June 1936. For two weeks before the rematch, Louis was quiet and withdrawn. Hours before the bout, he told his trainers, "I'm scared I might kill Schmeling tonight."

In the most politically charged sporting event ever held, 70,000 fans—some of whom had paid $100 for tickets—stirred in anticipation. Over a 100 million people worldwide tuned in on radio, including 20 million in Germany. Louis' strategy was to go for the kill immediately, and that he did.

With his powerful left, Louis jackhammered punches to Schmeling's face. "The blows

169

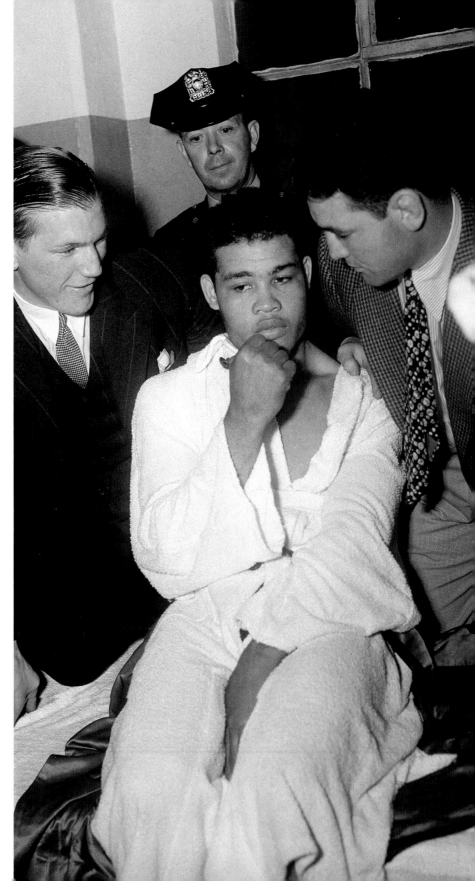

Louis' face remained unmarred after his quick dispatch of the Nazi poster boy. Joe would hold onto his heavyweight championship belt until 1949, long after the demise of the Third Reich.

tilted Max's head back, made his eyes blink, unquestionably stung him," *The New York Times* reported. "The German's head was going backward as if on hinges."

Three times Louis floored Schmeling in the first round, and after just two minutes and four seconds, the fight was over. Louis had avenged his one loss, exploded the myth of black inferiority, and struck a blow for freedom against the ugly face of fascism. "[W]hen the Germans learned how badly I was beating Schmeling, they cut the radio wires to Germany," Louis wrote. "They didn't want their people to know that just a plain old n——r was knocking the s——t out of the Aryan Race."

In Europe and the United States, people celebrated in different ways. The Jews of Germany rejoiced in secrecy, while black urbanites in America poured into the streets. In Harlem, the police cut off traffic from 125th to 145th Streets so that 100,000 African Americans could celebrate. "This is their night," the police commissioner told *The New York Times*. "Let them have their fun."

# Billy Graham's Bronx Crusade

July 20, 1957

When it became clear that worshippers would fill every seat in Yankee Stadium, guards allowed thousands to stand in the outfield. Thousands more couldn't even get into the building.

Nine months after Don Larsen's perfect game, New Yorkers ventured to Yankee Stadium expecting an even greater performance. Evangelist Billy Graham, who had enraptured the nation with his Christian revivals, was about to save souls from the stadium infield.

All New Yorkers were welcome, free of charge, and seemingly everyone came. Despite sweltering, 97-degree heat, every seat was filled by 6:30 P.M. for the 7:00 P.M. service. Ten minutes later, guards allowed the massive crowds outside the ballpark to enter the gates and fill up the outfield. Only the infield, encircled by a picket and wire fence, was off-limits to this sea of humanity. The crowd was estimated at 90,000 to 100,000—the largest gathering ever at Yankee Stadium.

Raised on a dairy farm in North Carolina, Graham became an ordained Southern Baptist minister in 1939. During World War II, his rousing sermons inspired servicemen in North America and Europe. He became a national sensation in 1949 with his Los Angeles crusade, in which overflow crowds swarmed a makeshift tent every night for two months. His subsequent radio program, "Hour of Decision," attracted huge audiences.

Graham saved souls with his London crusade in 1954, and in May 1957, he took on his greatest challenge to date: New York City. "I know that we are going to one of the strongholds of Satan," he wrote in his diary. For four months, Graham preached daily sermons to packed crowds at Madison Square Garden. "I am willing to give my life, ready to die in New York, to see a true spiritual revival in New York and America," he preached in early July.

On July 20, Graham appeared for one service only in Yankee Stadium—an event televised by ABC. A 3,000-member choir sang the "Hallelujah Chorus" and "How Great Thou Art." Vice President Richard Nixon and 300 others shared the platform with Graham, who preached, "Christ is the only answer to our problems and dilemmas." Around 9:00 P.M., Graham asked those who "accepted Christ" to stand up or raise their hands. Thousands obliged. By September 1, Graham concluded his New York crusade. Nearly two million people had attended his revivals, and—according to Graham's team—more than 56,000 pledged their lives to Christ.

# The Greatest Game of All

## December 28, 1958

Baltimore Colts fullback Alan Ameche bulls into the end zone in overtime—the first extra session ever played in the NFL. A national TV audience watched the thrilling championship game.

**Opposite Page:** Colts coach Weeb Ewbank addresses his team a day before they tore up the Yankee Stadium turf. The New York Giants played at the Stadium from 1956 to 1973.

Yankee Stadium hosted countless memorable moments in major-league history, but the historic stadium also helped launch the National Football League toward its future greatness when it hosted the NFL Championship Game, pitting the New York Giants against the Baltimore Colts.

In 1958, the NFL schedule contained just 12 games; the winner of each of the NFL's divisions qualified for the NFL Championship Game during that season. Baltimore earned its place in the championship after posting a 9-3 mark to win the Western Division. Johnny Unitas spearheaded a Colts offense that finished first in scoring. In the Eastern Division, the Cleveland Browns and the Giants had to play off to find a qualifier for the championship after each team finished with 9-3 records. After a 10-0 Giants win, the game was set. The Colts' high-powered offense would face the Giants' stellar defense that had allowed only 183 points, the fewest in the league.

With a national television audience soaking in this classic, the Giants led 17-14 late in the fourth quarter. Facing a third-and-four, Giants running back Frank Gifford was stopped short to force a punt. Still, the game looked over when the punt positioned the Colts 86 yards away from the Giants' end zone, with 1:56 showing on the clock.

Unitas then accomplished the improbable by methodically marching the Colts to the Giants' 13 with his passes. Seven seconds remained on the clock when Steve Myhra tied the game with a field goal to force "sudden death" overtime.

The Giants got the ball first and were stopped. Once again, a punt left the Colts facing a lengthy drive to score. But the Giants had no answer for Unitas, who drove his team 80 yards for the winning score, a one-yard touchdown plunge by fullback Alan Ameche.

The Colts' 23-17 victory was of epic proportions. It was among the first NFL games ever televised nationally, and it was the first overtime contest in league history. Due to those factors, along with the fourth-quarter theatrics, it became known as the Greatest Game Ever Played.

# Sermon on the Mound

## October 4, 1965

Pope Paul VI left Rome, landed in New York, said mass at St. Patrick's Cathedral, met with President Lyndon Johnson, spoke at the United Nations, recited mass at Yankee Stadium, visited a Harlem high school, spoke at the World's Fair, and flew back to Rome—all on the same day.

Over the years, Yankee Stadium hosted any number of events outside the baseball arena. One of the more interesting of these saw pinstripes give way to a papal miter, when the grand baseball cathedral made the conversion to an open-air Catholic church to host a pontifical mass for the visit of Pope Paul VI.

Yellow flags of the Vatican waved along with those of the United Nations for the occasion, and a picket fence was set up in front of the bleachers, designating an area for students. A red-carpeted dais sat in the center of the park, awaiting the pope's arrival.

Yankee Stadium's gates opened at 3:00 P.M. and the masses began to push through the turnstiles immediately. Crucifixes and rosaries were prominent among the crowd, many of whom carried blankets and extra clothing to combat the dropping temperatures, leading up to the start of the mass at 8:37 that night.

When Pope Paul VI arrived, he entered the ballpark in a convertible that drove through a gate in left field, the spot where members of the visiting team's bullpen entered the game to pitch to Yankees hitters. As expected, the night turned cold by the time the pope stepped to the dais, where a plain wood altar sat covered with a white linen cloth for the mass. Yankee Stadium swelled with more than 90,000 people of faith, hoping to be moved spiritually by the pope's message, along with others wanting to bring faith into their lives for the first time.

A humble man, the pope welcomed Catholics as well as those from other religions to the service. Speaking of peace and love, he told the crowd that peace needed to be rooted in moral and religious principles and must be alive in the conscience of mankind, as the Holy Scripture states.

Blessed by his presence, Yankee Stadium felt alive and holy that chilly October night.

# To the Moon, Norton!

## September 28, 1976

Ali (left) won over fans with his ability to avenge losses with triumphs in the rematches. "The Greatest" followed a loss to Ken Norton in 1973 with two wins in close decisions.

Ringside seats fetched $200. Upper-deck reserved spots sold for $25. More than 30,000 fans filed into Yankee Stadium to witness what turned out to be one of the most disputed decisions in the history of heavyweight boxing.

Ken Norton had shocked Muhammad Ali in March 1973, breaking his jaw, slowing Ali's ring comeback, and becoming just the second man to defeat "The Greatest." Later that year, Ali had avenged that loss by earning a tight decision against Norton, one of the most underrated athletes of his day. Ali had regained his title belt entering the "rubber match" with Norton in this cathedral of American sports venues.

Prior to this 15-round bout, Yankee Stadium had seen more than its share of great sports moments, but rarely had its patrons seen this much action packed into a single hour. Ali, who had chanted "Norton's gotta fall! Norton's gotta fall!" in predicting a win by knockout, used every trick he knew to try to deflate the challenger. He swung his arm, windmill-style. He rope-a-doped. He danced. He chirped at Norton throughout the match. Norton stood his ground.

Yankee Stadium's seats literally rocked as the combatants traded punch for punch several times during the fight. Norton, 20 months younger than the 34-year-old champion and in supreme physical shape, pummeled Ali's midsection so relentlessly that the champ appeared badly hurt during the fight's middle rounds. At the final bell, Norton was certain that he had won.

The scorecards, however, held a radically different view. Though Norton had carried the first part of the fight, the judges were in agreement in giving the final four rounds to the champ. The result: a unanimous decision for Ali—a decision that sent Norton's tears streaming to the ring, and one that *Boxing Monthly*, in 1998, ranked fifth on its list of the most disputed title decisions of all time.

# Honoring Victims and Heroes

## September 23, 2001

The event featured inspirational words from clergy of various faiths as well as musical performances, including Bette Midler (pictured) singing "Wind Beneath My Wings."

Just 12 days after the 9/11 terrorist attacks, Yankee Stadium hosted "A Prayer for America." Eddie Reardon of the Bronx was among the thousands who attended the ceremony amid heightened security. Under his arm, he carried the flag that had covered the casket of his father. Gus Reardon, who had died three years earlier, had been the head groundskeeper at Yankee Stadium.

"I wanted him to be here today," Eddie told the *Portland Press Herald*. Like the mourners in his company, it did not take much for Eddie to lose his composure. He burst into tears. "I wanted him to know that on this special day, I took his flag back to where he used to work.... He'd have been so proud of New York today."

This unprecedented event, staged on a pleasant Sunday afternoon, was meant to honor the victims and heroes of the recent tragedy and to help the city heal. "Closure" at this early stage was impossible. In fact, rescuers were still searching for bodies in the rubble of Ground Zero. But on this day, said attendee Katherine Muniz, "we can give lots of hugs and kisses and love."

Emotions ran the gamut during the three-hour ceremony, from solemnity and sadness to soaring joy and pride. The 15,000 who attended were offered roses and small American flags, while the American Red Cross contributed packets of tissues. Special guests—dignitaries, civil service workers, and victims' families—received stuffed animals with notes and drawings from American children. A bed of flowers lay at home plate, bunting lined the stadium, and a large stage was assembled in the outfield.

Bagpipers with the New York Police Department set the tone for the event with their rendition of "Amazing Grace." As former president Bill Clinton looked on, Oprah Winfrey and actor James Earl Jones served as hosts. "Today we offer a prayer for America," Jones intoned in his booming voice. "Our spirit is unbroken. In fact, it is stronger than ever."

Winfrey introduced a succession of speakers and musical artists, all of whom inspired those in attendance as well as a worldwide television audience. Mayor Rudy Giuliani, whose courage and leadership had kept the city strong for the past 12 days, earned the most raucous

175

ovation. "On September 11, New York City suffered the darkest day in our history," Giuliani said. "It's now up to us to make it its finest hour." Promising that "our skyline will rise again," the mayor added: "To those who say that our city will never be the same, I say you are right. It will be better."

Admiral Robert Natter, commander of the Atlantic Fleet, roused patriotic sentiment. In a message for the terrorists, he declared: "You picked the wrong city. You picked the wrong country." After country music star Lee Greenwood performed "God Bless the USA," the stirred masses waved their flags and chanted "USA! USA!"

At times, the crowd became solemn and subdued. Edward Cardinal Egan led the gathering in prayer. Other Christian, Jewish, and Muslim leaders spoke as well. Imam Izak-El M. Pasha pleaded, "Do not allow the ignorance of people to have you attack your good neighbors. We are Muslims, but we are Americans." As for the terrorists, he said, "they are no believers in God at all."

The sounding of a brass fire bell and the blowing of a shofar (ram's horn) followed each speech. So too did several extraordinary singing performances. Opera legend Placido Domingo touched souls with his rendition of "Ave Maria." The Harlem Boys and Girls Choir's version of "We Shall Overcome" was so moving that many in the crowd held hands and sang along.

In the most emotional performance of all, Bette Midler sang "Wind Beneath My Wings," a song that honors unrecognized heroes, such as the many New York firefighters and police officers who lost their lives. As Midler reached the song's soaring climax, many in the stands clutched their loved ones and wept uncontrollably. "Thank you!" Midler cried to the heavens. "Thank you!"

It would take years for the wounds of 9/11 to heal, but this special event at Yankee Stadium proved cathartic for all involved. As the American flag was raised to full-mast, many hoped that their deepest suffering was behind them. Christine Munson, who lost her mother in the tragedy, couldn't bear the thought of more pain and death. "My prayer today is that none of the rescuers get hurt," she said. "I don't want to lose anyone else."

## Speakers and Performers

In order of appearance:

- Rudy Washington, deputy mayor of New York City
- AmorArtis Chorus and Orchestra, singing "Battle Hymn of the Republic"
- James Earl Jones, actor
- Oprah Winfrey (master of ceremonies), talk show host
- Admiral Robert Natter, commander-in-chief of the Atlantic Fleet
- Ann Marie Maloney, Danny Rodriguez, and Kim Royster, New York City Police Department, singing the national anthem
- Edward Cardinal Egan, Archbishop of New York
- Rabbi Joseph Potasnik, New York Fire Department chaplain
- Rabbi Arthur Schneier
- Rabbi Alvin Kass, New York City Police Department chaplain
- Rabbi Marc Gellman, president of the New York Board of Rabbis
- Rabbi Joy Levitt
- Placido Domingo, singing "Ave Maria"
- Rudy Giuliani, mayor of New York City
- Griselda Cuevas, Incarnation Parish
- George Reece, New York City firefighter
- Rev. Thomas V. Daily, Bishop of Brooklyn
- Dr. Inderjit Singh, Sikh Temple in Richmond Hills
- Harlem Boys and Girls Choir, singing "Lift Every Voice and Sing" and "We Shall Overcome"
- George Pataki, governor of New York
- Imam Mohammad Shansay Ali
- Imam Mozi Ali
- Sister Zaimah Sabree
- Imam Fadre Ansari, Masjid Nu'man in Buffalo
- Imam Izak-El M. Pasha, NYPD chaplain
- Bette Midler, singing "Wind Beneath My Wings"
- Rev. Carolyn Holloway, DeWitt Reform Church of Manhattan
- Rt. Rev. Mark Sisk, Episcopal Bishop of New York
- Rev. James Forbes, Riverside Church
- Archbishop Anania Arapajian, Armenian Church in America
- Rev. Calvin Butts
- Rev. David Benke, president of the Atlantic District of the Lutheran Church
- Lee Greenwood, singing "God Bless the USA"
- Archbishop Demetrios, Greek Orthodox Church in America
- Pandit Roop Sukhram, Hindu Sreeraam Temple in Brooklyn
- Marc Anthony, singing "America the Beautiful"